WebAssembly for Cloud

A Basic Guide for Wasm-Based Cloud Apps

Shashank Mohan Jain

Apress®

WebAssembly for Cloud: A Basic Guide for Wasm-Based Cloud Apps

Shashank Mohan Jain
Bangalore, India

ISBN-13 (pbk): 978-1-4842-7495-8   ISBN-13 (electronic): 978-1-4842-7496-5
https://doi.org/10.1007/978-1-4842-7496-5

Managing Director, Apress Media LLC: Welmoed Spahr
Acquisitions Editor: Spandana Chatterjee
Coordinating Editor: Mark Powers

Cover designed by eStudioCalamar

Cover image by Jas Le on Unsplash (www.unsplash.com)

Distributed to the book trade worldwide by Apress Media, LLC, 1 New York Plaza, New York, NY 10004, U.S.A. Phone 1-800-SPRINGER, fax (201) 348-4505, e-mail orders-ny@ springer-sbm.com, or visit www.springeronline.com. Apress Media, LLC is a California LLC and the sole member (owner) is Springer Science + Business Media Finance Inc (SSBM Finance Inc). SSBM Finance Inc is a **Delaware** corporation.

For information on translations, please e-mail booktranslations@springernature.com; for reprint, paperback, or audio rights, please e-mail bookpermissions@springernature.com.

Apress titles may be purchased in bulk for academic, corporate, or promotional use. eBook versions and licenses are also available for most titles. For more information, reference our Print and eBook Bulk Sales web page at http://www.apress.com/bulk-sales.

Any source code or other supplementary material referenced by the author in this book is available to readers on GitHub via the book's product page, located at www.apress.com/9781484274958. For more detailed information, please visit http://www.apress.com/source-code.

Printed on acid-free paper

I dedicate this book to my parents and their blessings, without which this book was not at all possible.

I also dedicate this book to my dear wife. I would not have been able to write it without her constant pushing and support.

I appreciate my angel of a daughter for allowing me the time to write this book.

Finally, I thank a dear friend who constantly pushed me into writing this.

Table of Contents

About the Author

Shashank Mohan Jain has worked in the IT industry for 20 years, mainly in cloud computing and distributed systems. He has a keen interest in virtualization techniques, security, and complex systems.

Shashank has more then 30 software patents in cloud computing, IoT, and machine learning. He has been a speaker at many cloud conferences. In addition, he holds Sun, Microsoft, and Linux kernel certifications.

About the Technical Reviewer

Srinivasa Reddy Challa is an expert developer at SAP. He has experience developing applications in various programming languages, including Java, Kotlin, Node.js, Rust, Golang, and Python, and frameworks like Spring, Django, and Express. Srinivasa also has extensive experience working with cloud providers like AWS, Azure, and AliCloud and has cloud certification in AWS. He has a bachelor's degree in computer science engineering.

Acknowledgments

I would like to acknowledge Kevin Hoffman, whose work in WebAssembly is an inspiration. Kevin is the creator of the waPC library, which is used in a chapter in the book.

Introduction

Somewhere, something incredible is waiting to be known.

—Carl Sagan

I start this journey with a quote from the eminent scientist and science communicator Carl Sagan. This short book introduces the amazing world of WebAssembly. The book's main theme is to create a simple WebAssembly program from scratch and take it to the cloud. In doing this, you'll gain a solid introduction to the valuable features offered by WebAssembly. Consider this book an introduction to WebAssembly and how it is powering browser-based applications and cloud applications. 'To get the most out of this book, you should have a bit of understanding of cloud fundamentals and basic knowledge of programming languages like Rust, golang and javascript.'

CHAPTER 1

WebAssembly Introduction

Before introducing WebAssembly, it's important to get a brief history of virtualization to better understand the context of WebAssembly.

When VMware started the virtualization revolution, virtual machines were positioned as the unit of computation. This meant that you could create and deploy software compatible with a virtual machine (VM). The VM-based approach provided great isolation because it introduced a kernel boundary between software and the host on which the workload ran (called a *hypervisor*). Although they were secure, VMs were heavy in nature and took time to spin up.

As cloud technology progressed, we saw the advent of *container-based virtualization*, which was mainly facilitated by structures within the Linux kernel. Containers on the same host shared the Linux kernel but have adequate mechanisms for security, like namespaces, seccomp profiles, and SELinux, which offered multilayered security for containers. In 2018, a new technology called WebAssembly has emerged. It was created by Mozilla and started as a browser-based technology. Since then, developers have employed it on the cloud and server-side apps. WebAssembly allows an extra level of virtualization by running the Wasm computation within a Linux process.

Things began with virtual machines (which are complete operating systems) and then moved to Linux containers (Linux processes protected and isolated by the Linux kernel). Now there is WebAssembly,

© Shashank Mohan Jain 2022
S. M. Jain, *WebAssembly for Cloud*, https://doi.org/10.1007/978-1-4842-7496-5_1

a computation unit within the Linux process. The goal is to provide a computation unit that can quickly spin up and be suitable for serverless workloads.

WebAssembly (also known as Wasm) is the new universal bytecode for interoperable compute units. *Interoperable* means that the compute unit should be able to run on any compatible Wasm runtime. A *compute unit* is a Wasm module. The basic idea is to have a bytecode format that is universal and standard.

Languages like JavaScript, Rust, Golang, and Java can be compiled to a Wasm-based bytecode. Once this bytecode is generated, it can be executed on any Wasm runtime.

Wasm is a small and efficient stack-based virtual machine that abstracts the target architecture by compiling the code to a universal bytecode representation. Wasm is based on an industry-wide collaborative effort to get a performant and secure close to assembly language. The Bytecode Alliance, set up to create shared implementations of WebAssembly standards, includes major players like Arm, Intel, Google, Microsoft, Mozilla, and Fastly.

Wasm is also well suited to run code in a multitenant way because it has the right security primitives built into it. Since it's launched within a process but is not a process itself, it also provides a means to avoid cold start problems, which are typical of serverless environments. Wasm is gaining tractions in areas like

- Providing data filtering capabilities in case of gateways like Envoy

- Policy engines like Open Policy Agent

- Kubernetes admission controller

- Databases like Postgres with custom extensions supporting Wasm

Wasm is now seen as a forefront technology in the cloud-native community. According to the Cloud Native Computing Foundation's CTO, Chris Aniszczyk, "Any project that has an extension mechanism will probably take advantage of Wasm to do that."

> *The promise, and excitement, is around a mix of portability and speed.*
>
> —Fintan Ryan, a senior analyst at Gartner

With low resource overhead and speed up in startup time compared to JavaScript, Wasm can be provisioned on IoT devices with resource-constrained memory, CPU, and storage. With no cold start issues, the portability and low resource consumption would make WebAssembly ideal for serverless deployments on the cloud and the edge. Initially started as a sandboxing technique for browser-based applications (for example, running image processing, decoding video and audio on the browser), it has now made inroads into server-side technologies due to powerful sandboxing capabilities and low overhead.

The security capabilities of Wasm make it a good fit for preventing security vulnerabilities like buffer overflows and control flow integrity issues. Wasm separates code and data. It has a static type system with type checking and a very structured control flow designed to make it easier to write code that compiles to be safe, with linear memory, global variables, and stack memory accessed separately. These aspects are discussed in the later chapters in regards to how Wasm provides neat mechanisms to avoid such security challenges.

Under the hood, Wasm runtime is a stack-based virtual machine operating on the Wasm bytecode by pushing and popping data off the stack. The closest comparison would be to the working of a JVM. One major difference is that JVM bytecode isn't universal (i.e., only programming languages like Kotlin and Scala can be compiled as Java bytecode). But, almost all the programming languages like C, C++, Rust, Golang, and JavaScript can be compiled into Wasm bytecode.

Wasm currently only supports numeric data types, although there's a proposal to add reference types like strings, sequences, records, variants to make it easier for Wasm modules to interact with modules running in other runtimes or written in different languages. Though this is not a limitation, other data types, such as strings, can still be realized with these numeric types, just that it makes programming Wasm directly a bit tedious. A Wasm module doesn't have access to APIs and system calls in the OS. If you want it to interact with anything outside the module, you must explicitly import it, so the only code that could be executed is the code that is packaged as part of the module. This interaction with the operating system calls is facilitated by a new spec known as WASI (WebAssembly System Interface). The WASI spec allows an interoperable Wasm code that can be ported to any Wasm runtime (i.e., runtimes like Lucet, Wasmer, and Node.js) once the Wasm compiler generates the bytecode.

Wasm in the Cloud

There are differences in running Wasm in a browser vs. running it on a cloud or an edge application (e.g., on an IoT device). When running Wasm on a browser, the interface to the OS is handled by the browser on behalf of the Wasm module. For servers or edge applications, this must be facilitated by the Wasm runtime hosting the Wasm module. The types of system calls would be like a file system I/O or network I/O.

One approach was to have each hosting Wasm runtime implement how to facilitate the system call on behalf of the Wasm module. This was the approach so far, but this led to portability issues as each runtime exposes different methods for the Wasm module to consume for making the system calls. The WASI spec evolved in the Wasm community to provide standardization. It's a modular set of system interfaces that looks like an abstracted OS, with low-level interfaces like I/O and high-level interfaces like cryptography, keeping WebAssembly code portable. This also provided better security as with this fine-grained access control can be achieved. For example, a certain Wasm module can only access certain files and not the whole file system. This considerably reduces the possible attack surface originating from a specific Wasm module, even if it's malicious.

Many runtimes have emerged to support running Wasm-based workloads in the cloud and edge. Node.js is a prominent player with the V8 runtime supporting the execution of the Wasm modules by loading them within JavaScript code. The Bytecode Alliance had three runtimes. Two (Wasmtime and Fastly's Lucet) recently merged, optimizing edge compute using ahead-of-time compilation to reduce latency. It is rewritten on top of Wasmtime. WAMR, the micro runtime, is for embedded devices with limited resources; that remains a separate runtime.

There are other runtimes, such as Wasmer and TeaVM (for Java bytecode to Wasm). As the community grows, and thereby the number of runtimes grows, it becomes important to keep an eye on the performance aspects of these runtimes. There is a set of benchmarks that measure different aspects of Wasm's runtime performance.

Figure 1-1 shows that the wavm runtime is fastest, followed by the node runtime.

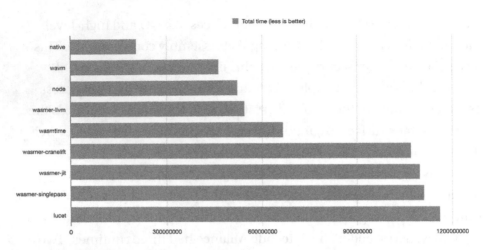

Figure 1-1. *Wasm runtime performance*

Figure 1-2 shows the performance aspects where again wavm is the fastest, followed by the node runtime.

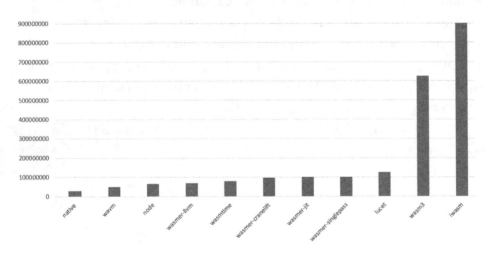

Figure 1-2. *Wasm runtime performance (interpreted mode)*

The following are the main benefits of using WebAssembly.

- Near-native performance

- Lightweight

- Security

- Easy debugging

- Hardware, language, and platform-independent

The following are the eight objects that are key to WebAssembly.

- WebAssembly.Module contains stateless WebAssembly code that has been pre-compiled by the browser.

- WebAssemly.Global represents a global variable instance that is accessible from both JavaScript and is importable/exportable across one or more instances of WebAssembly.Module.

- WebAssembly.Instance is a stateful, executable instance of WebAssembly.Module.

- WebAssembly.Memory is a resizable ArrayBuffer or SharedArrayBuffer that holds raw bytes of memory accessed by a WebAssembly.Instance.

- WebAssembly.Table a JavaScript wrapper that stores function references.

- WebAssembly.CompileError indicates an error during decoding or validation.

- WebAssembly.LinkError indicates an error during a module instantiation.

- WebAssembly.RuntimeError is an error that is thrown when WebAssembly specifies a trap.

Chapter 2 goes into more detail.

WebAssembly Use Cases

There are so many use cases for WebAssembly. The following are some of the possibilities.

- Greenfield/multiplatform development

- Serverless development

- Database plugins written in Wasm for triggers

- Serving complete servers like Node.js within browsers like WebContainers

- Migrating from desktop-only to desktop and browser-based applications (AutoCAD and games)

- Progressive web apps

- Mobile apps

There are many other use cases.

WebAssembly Architecture

At a high level, the diagram in Figure 1-3 shows how WebAssembly works. The left side of Figure 1-3 lists languages like Rust, Golang, C, and C++ that compile them to WebAssembly, which is then deployed on a Wasm virtual machine. The Wasm virtual machine executes the Wasm module by converting it into target hardware-specific machine code.

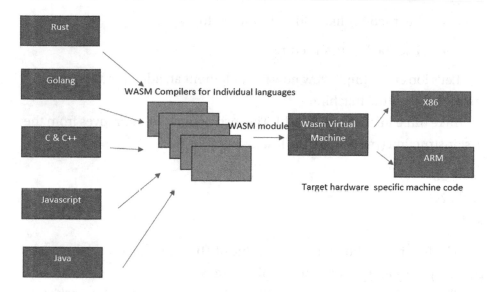

Figure 1-3. *High-level architecture of WebAssembly framework*

It becomes evident from Figure 1-3, the goal of WebAssembly is to be a universal bytecode. This means that software written in different languages can be compiled in a Wasm format and be executed on a WebAssembly virtual machine.

Stack-Based Virtual Machine

The WebAssembly virtual machine is implemented as a stack-based virtual machine. A stack-based virtual machine emulates a real CPU.

Let's take an example of a simple stack-based virtual machine for performing simple calculations like addition, subtraction, and multiplication.

The following are four things that work on such a machine.

- The stack pointer, which points to the top of the stack

- The instruction pointer, which points to the next instruction

- Instructions like add, sub, and multiply

- The stack data structure

Let's look at a simple flow now to implement an add operation on a stack-based virtual machine.

Take three instructions to add. The instruction pointer moves from the first instruction (push 10) to the last instruction, add.

```
push 10
push 20
add
```

The first instruction pushes the value of 10 on the stack, and the stack pointer points to that value on top of the stack.

The second instruction pushes 20 as the value on top of the stack, and the stack pointer now points to that.

The Wasm runtime implements the add instruction to get the two values from the stack, adds them, and pushes the result back to the stack.

The subtract and multiply instructions are implemented on another line.

The following are the textual format of the code snippets for the WebAssembly module to perform addition, subtraction, multiplication. Don't worry about the syntax; it is explained in Chapter 2.

```
(func (param $a i32) (param $b i32) (result i32)
    get_local $a
    get_local $b
    i32.add
)
(func (param $a i32) (param $b i32) (result i32)
    get_local $a
    get_local $b
    i32.sub
)
```

```
(func (param $a i32) (param $b i32) (result i32)
   get_local $a
   get_local $b
   i32.mul
)
```

There are three function definitions (add, subtract and multiply) within a WebAssembly module.

The following are the three instructions.

```
get_local $a
get_local $b
i32.add
get_local $a pushes the value of parameter a on the stack
get_local $b pushes the value of parameter b on the stack
```

i32.add pops these two values, performs an addition, and pushes the result back on the stack.

In simple terms, this is how a WebAssembly stack-based virtual machine works.

Summary

This chapter briefly looked at virtualization and where WebAssembly fits into it. You learned about WebAssembly and its architecture. You saw how different WebAssembly runtimes compare to each other in terms of performance.

You also looked at a stack-based virtual machine and how a WebAssembly virtual machine implements a stack-based virtual machine to run Wasm bytecode.

CHAPTER 2

WebAssembly Module Internals: Sections and Memory Model

This chapter explains what constitutes a WebAssembly module and shows you what its memory model looks like. It discusses how the different sections of the WebAssembly module are structured and the significance of each section.

Figure 2-1 shows the structure of a Wasm file.

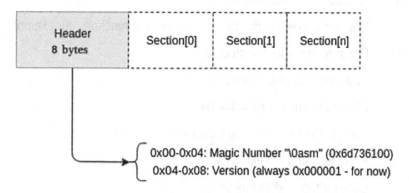

Figure 2-1. *Structure of a WebAssembly file*

© Shashank Mohan Jain 2022

S. M. Jain, *WebAssembly for Cloud*, https://doi.org/10.1007/978-1-4842-7496-5_2

The WebAssembly header is an 8-byte filled with the magic number \0asm in ASCII.

It is followed by the version number, which is always 1.

The hex representation "\x00\x61\x73\x6d\x01\x00\x00\x00" represents the 0asm magic number and the version combined. This is needed to create a valid Wasm file.

On an Ubuntu machine, type the following command.

```
printf "\x00\x61\x73\x6d\x01\x00\x00\x00" > test.wasm
```

This creates a valid Wasm file called test.wasm, which any of the Wasm runtimes can load.

The different Wasm module sections are listed in Table 2-1.

Table 2-1. *Wasm Module Sections*

Section	Description
Type	Declares unique function signatures
Import	Declares imports
Function	Functions used within a module
Table	Used for indirection by storing references to functions, for example
Memory	Linear memory for the module
Global	Declaration of global variables
Export	All exported functions to the host
Start	Index to the function to be called at the start of a module
Element	Initializes imported modules
Code	Code for the module functions
Data	Data to be loaded in the linear memory during initialization
Custom	Any other kinds of custom data

There are 12 sections in a single Wasm module, with each having a specific purpose.

Each section has a header with a unique code that describes the type of the section (i.e., if it's a type, import, or function, etc.) and a payload component that contains the payload of the section. Only one section can have one code within a Wasm module.

Figure 2-2 shows an example of section headers.

```
Sections:

     Type start=0x0000000a end=0x00000011 (size=0x00000007) count: 1
 Function start=0x00000013 end=0x00000017 (size=0x00000004) count: 3
   Export start=0x00000019 end=0x00000036 (size=0x0000001d) count: 3
     Code start=0x00000038 end=0x00000051 (size=0x00000019) count: 3
```

Figure 2-2. *Section headers*

Each section header depicts the start and end of the section and its size.

Figure 2-3 shows some of the sections from a Wasm file.

```
Section Details:

Type[1]:
 - type[0] (i32, i32) -> i32
Function[3]:
 - func[0] sig=0 <add>
 - func[1] sig=0 <subtract>
 - func[2] sig=0 <multiply>
Export[3]:
 - func[0] <add> -> "add"
 - func[1] <subtract> -> "subtract"
 - func[2] <multiply> -> "multiply"
Code[3]:
 - func[0] size=7 <add>
 - func[1] size=7 <subtract>
 - func[2] size=7 <multiply>
```

Figure 2-3. *Sections of the Wasm file*

Figure 2-3 shows that the type section has one type, which takes two 32-bit integers as input and returns a 32-bit integer.

In the function section, you see three functions, and since there is only one type defined, all three functions are of the same type (signatures). sig=0 in the function body points to type[0] where the signature is defined. All three take two 32-bit integers as input and return a 32-bit integer as output.

The export section shows which functions are exported out of the Wasm module for the host to invoke. In this case, all three functions are exported to the host.

The code section constitutes the actual code instructions for the functions.

Each section consists of the following.

- A one-byte section ID

- The i32 (4 bytes) *size* of the contents, in bytes (each section can have approximately 4 GB of size)

- The actual *contents* of the section (for most sections, it's a vector representation)

Each section has a specific ID. As per WebAssembly specs, Table 2-2 lists the section IDs.

Table 2-2. *Sections and Their IDs*

ID	Section
0	custom section
1	type section
2	import section
3	function section
4	table section

(continued)

Table 2-2. (*continued*)

ID	Section
5	memory section
6	global section
7	export section
8	start section
9	element section
10	code section
11	data section
12	data count section

Type Section

The type section defines the unique signatures of the functions defined in the Wasm module, which specify the following.

- The input parameters and their types

- The return type of the function

Table 2-3 shows examples of this section.

Table 2-3. *Type Section*

Index	Type
0	(i32) (i32) -> (i32)
1	(i64) -> ()
2	(i64) (i64) -> ()

17

The first type specifies a signature that takes two 32-bit integers as input parameters and returns a 32-bit integer.

The second type specifies a signature that takes a 64-bit integer as input and returns a void, and finally, the third type specifies a signature that takes two 64-bit integers as input and returns a void.

Function Section

The function section specifies the type of functions being used in the specific module. For example, if there are three functions in a module as defined in Table 2-4. The types listed in Table 2-4 are referred from the types in Table 2-2.

Table 2-4. *Function Section*

Index	Function
0	Type 0
1	Type 2
2	Type 1

Table 2-4 depicts a function section. For example, the first function of type 0 takes two 32-bit integers as input and returns a 32-bit integer as a return type, and similarly, for other functions, the signatures are mapped to a specific type.

Code Section

The code section constitutes the actual function implementation, as shown in Table 2-5.

Table 2-5. *Code Section*

Index	Function Code
0	Code for 0th function
1	Code for 1st function
2	Code for 2nd function

The function section index points to the index of the code section.

Figure 2-4 is an example of a simple Wasm module and shows a code section.

```
Code Disassembly:

00003a func[0] <add>:
 00003b: 20 00                    | local.get 0
 00003d: 20 01                    | local.get 1
 00003f: 6a                       | i32.add
 000040: 0b                       | end
000042 func[1] <subtract>:
 000043: 20 00                    | local.get 0
 000045: 20 01                    | local.get 1
 000047: 6b                       | i32.sub
 000048: 0b                       | end
00004a func[2] <multiply>:
 00004b: 20 00                    | local.get 0
 00004d: 20 01                    | local.get 1
 00004f: 6c                       | i32.mul
 000050: 0b                       | end
```

Figure 2-4. *Code sections of the Wasm file*

You can see several instructions use local.get 0 and similar operations. They are primarily stack-related operations. Since Wasm is a stack-based virtual machine, the instructions in Wasm work on pushing and popping values to the stack. This is covered in Chapter 3, where you start to implement the Wasm module by hand.

Export Section

The export section defines the exports in specific Wasm modules; for example, you want to expose a function defined within a Wasm module to the Wasm runtime. Exports become visible to the host machine. Wasm also allows you to export the memory and data sections of a module.

Here is how an export will look like

Figure 2-5 shows an export.

```
Export[3]:
  - func[0] <add> -> "add"
  - func[1] <subtract> -> "subtract"
  - func[2] <multiply> -> "multiply"
```

Figure 2-5. *Exports of the Wasm file*

There are three functions exported out of the Wasm module. These three functions are available to the Wasm runtime (for example, Node.js) to invoke these functions.

Import Section

The import section defines the import functions from other Wasm modules or the host. Chapter 3 showcases an example of a function on a Node.js-based Wasm runtime invoked from within a Wasm module.

Table Section

The table section provides a level of indirection for functions. This is like a mapping of a virtual index to the reference to actual function code. Any invocation happens via this table mapping rather than having a direct reference to the function code. Any code doesn't have access to the direct function pointers in this case and provides a security feature to avoid manipulating an instruction pointer to some malicious code. Whenever a function is invoked, the WebAssembly framework intercepts and looks at the table, and invokes the actual function.

The table is initialized with a specific size. The number of entries in a table can increase. A table can also be capped by a maximum number. If a maximum number of entries is not configured, it is an unbounded table.

Figure 2-6 is an example of a Wasm with a table section.

```
Type[2]:
 - type[0] (i32, i32) -> i32
 - type[1] (i32, i32, i32) -> i32
Function[4]:
 - func[0] sig=0
 - func[1] sig=0
 - func[2] sig=0
 - func[3] sig=1 <callByIndex>
Table[1]:
 - table[0] type=funcref initial=3
Export[1]:
 - func[3] <callByIndex> -> "callByIndex"
Elem[1]:
 - segment[0] flags=0 table=0 count=3 - init i32=0
  - elem[0] = func[0]
  - elem[1] = func[1]
  - elem[2] = func[2]
Code[4]:
 - func[0] size=7
 - func[1] size=7
 - func[2] size=7
 - func[3] size=11 <callByIndex>
```

Figure 2-6. *Table section in the Wasm module*

The table section in Figure 2-6 has one function specified with a funcref element.

Memory Section

From a security standpoint, the memory section is one of the most important sections. It is represented as linear memory and instantiated by the host as an array. In the Wasm module, it's just like normal memory, which is linear. The Wasm runtime intercepts memory access to keep it in bounds. The framework disallows anything outside the bounds. This mechanism allows you to do memory sandboxing within a Linux process. This lets you run each tenant workload within its own Wasm module within one Linux process.

Memory for a module is structured in pages as it's structured in a Linux process. (The default page size in Linux is 4K but is configurable.) The only difference here is that the page size for a Wasm module is 64K. The Wasm runtime provisions this memory to the Wasm module in the number of pages. These pages can be dynamically increased to the max size if specified. Apart from providing sandboxing, sometimes modules are required to share memory similar to IPC (inter-process communication) semantics. WebAssembly allows two modules to have a shared memory setup if needed.

The following is a memory segment in a Wasm file.

```
(memory (export "memory") 1 4)
```

This would mean provision the Wasm module with the memory of a single page and expandable up to four pages. The memory can be expanded on invocation of the memory.grow function by the Wasm runtime. This is limited by the max number of pages of memory for a Wasm module, however.

Normally in programs written in C or C++, there was the possibility of attacks by manipulating the instruction pointer, mainly due to the execution stack being part of the process memory. This allowed developers to craft attacks like buffer overflow, stack smashing, and so forth. Although many of them have been mitigated by mechanisms like *address space randomized layout* (ASRL), architectures like Wasm separate the execution stack from memory for data, thereby making these attacks almost impossible.

An example of a memory section with the memory of a single page is shown in Figure 2-7.

```
Type[2]:
 - type[0] (i32, i32) -> nil
 - type[1] () -> nil
Import[2]:
 - func[0] sig=0 <example.log> <- example.log
 - memory[0] pages: initial=1 <- js.mem
Function[1]:
 - func[1] sig=1 <logme>
Export[1]:
 - func[1] <logme> -> "logme"
Code[1]:
 - func[1] size=8 <logme>
```

Figure 2-7. *Memory section*

There are two ways to create a memory for a WebAssembly module.

- Within the module using it in a Wasm module (memory 1)

- Provisioned via the embedding host, such as a JavaScript engine (Some of the information shown in Figure 2-7 is explained in later chapters.)

Data Section

The data section allows initializing some data during the initialization of the WebAssembly module; for example, certain configurations can be loaded into the data section if needed.

The following is a data section in a module.

```
(data (i32.const 0) "Hello Wat")
```

Figure 2-8 shows how the data section initializes a "Hello Wat" string in the linear memory of the Wasm module.

```
Section Details:

Type[2]:
 - type[0] (i32, i32) -> nil
 - type[1] () -> nil
Import[2]:
 - func[0] sig=0 <example.log> <- example.log
 - memory[0] pages: initial=1 <- js.mem
Function[1]:
 - func[1] sig=1 <logme>
Export[1]:
 - func[1] <logme> -> "logme"
Code[1]:
 - func[1] size=8 <logme>
Data[1]:
 - segment[0] memory=0 size=9 - init i32=0
  - 0000000: 4865 6c6c 6f20 5761 74              Hello Wat
```

Figure 2-8. *Data section*

The host can read from the location and offset the linear memory to get this string. This is one way that allows guest-to-host communication is explained in Chapter 3.

You can also see the hex representation in the last line in Figure 2-8 is equivalent to the "Hello Wat" text representation.

```
4865 6c6c 6f20 5761 74
H e  l l  o    W a  t
```

Custom Section

You have seen that the data section can store arbitrary strings in Wasm. The custom section allows you to make this mechanism more extensible by storing more things within custom sections. It can be module metadata-related information or information.

Start Section

The start section points to the index of the starting function to be invoked when the execution starts. People familiar with the C main function can draw a parallel here.

Global Section

The global section holds the global variables of the Wasm module and specifies if a variable is mutable or not.

Programmatically Parsing a Wasm File

Let's discuss using a Golang-based program to parse through the Wasm file and print the different sections of a specific Wasm file. The following explains the prerequisites to do this.

1. Install Golang 1.16 and set up GOROOT, GOPATH, and other environment variables.

2. Create a wasm_parser directory.

3. In the directory, create a main.go file.

4. Copy the following code.

Listing 2-1. Parsing Wasm Module

```
1.   package main
2.   import (
3.   "flag"
4.   "fmt"
5.   "os"
6.   "text/tabwriter"
7.   wasm "github.com/akupila/go-wasm"
8.   )

9.   func main() {
10.  file := flag.String("file", "", "file to parse (.wasm)")
11.  flag.Parse()

12.  if *file == "" {
     a.    flag.Usage()
     b.    os.Exit(2)
13.  }

14.  f, err := os.Open(*file)
15.  if err != nil {
     a.    fmt.Fprintf(os.Stderr, "open file: %v", err)
     b.    os.Exit(1)
16.  }
17.  defer f.Close()

18.  mod, err := wasm.Parse(f)
19.  if err != nil {
     a.    fmt.Fprintln(os.Stderr, err)
     b.    os.Exit(1)
20.  }

21.  w := tabwriter.NewWriter(os.Stdout, 0, 0, 4, ' ', 0)
22.  fmt.Fprintf(w, "Index\tName\tSize (bytes)\n")
```

```
23.  for i, s := range mod.Sections {
        a.   fmt.Fprintf(w, "%d\t%s\t%d\n", i, s.Name(),
        s.Size())
24.  }
25.  w.Flush()
26.  }
```

In the wasm_parser directory, run the following commands.

```
go get github.com/akupila/go-wasm/
go mod init main.go
go mod tidy
```

This generates two files: go.mod and go.sum.

Once this is done, you can build the code using the following command.

```
go build -o wasm_parser
```

This generates an executable named wasm_parser.

To execute this binary, use the calc.wasm file built in previous sections of this chapter.

Execute the following binary.

```
./wasm_parser --file calc.wasm
```

The sections of the module print, as shown in Figure 2-9.

```
ubuntu@INLN34327424A:~/wasm_parser$ ./wasm_parser --file ../wat/calc.wasm
Index    Name       Size (bytes)
0        Type       7
1        Function   4
2        Export     29
3        Code       25
```

Figure 2-9. *Sections of the calc Wasm module*

Let's look at a different Wasm file with more sections and run the same command.

Use the string.wasm file built in previous sections of this chapter.

Executing the following command results in the output shown in Figure 2-10.

```
./wasm_parser --file string.wasm
```

```
ubuntu@INLN34327424A:~/wasm_parser$ ./wasm_parser --file ../wat/string.wasm
Index     Name        Size (bytes)
0         Type        9
1         Import      25
2         Function    2
3         Export      9
4         Code        10
5         Data        15
```

Figure 2-10. *Sections of the Wasm module string*

Note that the import and data sections are now in the module.

Next, let's modify the code to print the code sections of the two Wasm modules. Add the following code segment after line number 25 in Listing 2-1.

Listing 2-2. Listing Section Code and Section Bodies

```
1.   for j, s := range mod.Sections {
2.   _=j
3.   switch section := s.(type) {
4.   case *wasm.SectionCode:
5.   // can now read function bytecode from section.
6.   //       fmt.Println(section.Bodies)

7.   for i := 0; i < len(section.Bodies); i++ {
8.   fmt.Println("function code ",section.Bodies[i].Code)
9.   }
10.  }
11.  }
```

28

This code iterates over the code segment of the Wasm module. It iterates over the code bodies of each function and prints the bytecode of each function.

Code bytes for Wasm module calc.wasm

```
ubuntu@INLN34327424A:~/wasm_parser$ ./wasm_parser --file ../wat/calc.wasm
function code  [32 0 32 1 106 11]
function code  [32 0 32 1 107 11]
function code  [32 0 32 1 108 11]
```

Figure 2-11. *Bytecode for the function in calc.wasm*

Code bytes for Wasm module string.wasm

```
ubuntu@INLN34327424A:~/wasm_parser$ ./wasm_parser --file ../wat/string.wasm
function code  [65 0 65 9 16 0 11]
```

Figure 2-12. *Bytecode for function in string.wasm*

To inspect the exported functions, add the following code section to main.go. The code must be clubbed to the updated Listing 2-2 after line 3.

Listing 2-3. Listing Section Entries

```go
case *wasm.SectionExport:

for i := 0; i < len(section.Entries); i++ {
        fmt.Println("export function field ",section.
        Entries[i].Field)
}
```

Figure 2-13 shows the calc.wasm output.

```
ubuntu@INLN34327424A:~/wasm_parser$ ./wasm_parser --file ../wat/calc.wasm
export function field  add
export function field  subtract
export function field  multiply
```

Figure 2-13. *Exports section for calc.wasm*

Since only one function is exported for string.wasm, you see the output
shown in Figure 2-14.

```
ubuntu@INLN34327424A:~/wasm_parser$ ./wasm_parser --file ../wat/string.wasm
export function field  logme
```

Figure 2-14. *Exports section for string.wasm*

Chapter 3 discusses these Wasm files in more detail.

Next, let's look at the type section via this program.

Add the following code section to the main.go file to print the type
information of the Wasm file.

```
case *wasm.SectionType:

for i := 0; i < len(section.Entries); i++ {

        fmt.Println("type form field ",section.Entries[i].Form)
        fmt.Println("type Params field ",section.Entries[i].
        Params)
        fmt.Println("type return type field ",section.
        Entries[i].ReturnTypes)
}
```

After executing the code, the type information is printed (see Figure 2-15).
Signature type of all the functions defined in this Wasm module is the same
(see Figure 2-16).

```
ubuntu@INLN34327424A:~/wasm_parser$ ./wasm_parser --file ../wat/calc.wasm
type form field  96
type Params field  [127 127]
type return type field  [127]
```

Figure 2-15. *Type section for calc.wasm*

```
ubuntu@INLN34327424A:~/wasm_parser$ ./wasm_parser --file ../wat/string.wasm
type form field  96
type Params field  [127 127]
type return type field  []
type form field  96
type Params field  []
type return type field  []
```

Figure 2-16. *Type section for string.wasm*

You see that string.wasm has two different function signatures.

The first function takes two int32 as input and returns a void, while the second function takes no parameters and returns void.

Summary

This chapter looked at the internals of a WebAssembly module and how the different sections in a module are laid out. You also learned the importance of each section, like functions, table, memory, types, and data. Finally, you learned how to programmatically parse through the Wasm file and extract the needed section information from the Wasm file.

WebAssembly Text Toolkit and Other Utilities

The WebAssembly text toolkit is a toolkit to peek into a Wasm module in a textual format. Although the Wasm module is binary, this toolkit allows you to convert Wasm into a human-readable text format.

This chapter looks at some of the utilities that allow you to do the following.

- Create a text file in WebAssembly text format (wat) and generate a Wasm file from it

- Generate a wat file from a Wasm file

- Generate a dump of the Wasm file

The wat2wasm Utility

This tool handcrafts Wasm files in a text format and then generates the actual Wasm file. Since this is a human-readable format, it allows for a deeper understanding of the Wasm layout under the hood.

© Shashank Mohan Jain 2022
S. M. Jain, *WebAssembly for Cloud*, https://doi.org/10.1007/978-1-4842-7496-5_3

It is a handy tool for beginners to WebAssembly. This chapter features a few examples of a wat file and shows you how to generate a Wasm file and then load it via a Node.js-based Wasm runtime.

```
Pre requisites
Git and Ubuntu VM
Cmake
sudo apt-get update && sudo apt-get install build-essential
```

Clone the WebAssembly Binary Toolkit (WABT) repository.

```
git clone --recursive https://github.com/WebAssembly/wabt
cd wabt
git submodule update --init
```

Once you have downloaded the WABT repo, it's time to build the source.

```
mkdir build
cd build
cmake ..
```

Figure 3-1 is the build screenshot for the WABT make process.

```
cmake --build .
```

```
root@INLN34327424A:/home/ubuntu/wabt/build# cmake ..
-- The CXX compiler identification is GNU 9.3.0
-- Check for working CXX compiler: /usr/bin/c++
-- Check for working CXX compiler: /usr/bin/c++ -- works
-- Detecting CXX compiler ABI info
-- Detecting CXX compiler ABI info - done
-- Detecting CXX compile features
-- Detecting CXX compile features - done
-- Looking for alloca.h
-- Looking for alloca.h - found
-- Looking for unistd.h
-- Looking for unistd.h - found
-- Looking for snprintf
-- Looking for snprintf - found
-- Looking for strcasecmp
-- Looking for strcasecmp - found
-- Looking for sys/types.h
-- Looking for sys/types.h - found
-- Looking for stdint.h
-- Looking for stdint.h - found
-- Looking for stddef.h
-- Looking for stddef.h - found
-- Check size of ssize_t
-- Check size of ssize_t - done
-- Check size of size_t
-- Check size of size_t - done
-- Found PythonInterp: /usr/bin/python3 (found suitable version "3.8.5", minimum required is "3.5")
-- Looking for pthread.h
-- Looking for pthread.h - found
-- Performing Test CMAKE_HAVE_LIBC_PTHREAD
-- Performing Test CMAKE_HAVE_LIBC_PTHREAD - Failed
-- Looking for pthread_create in pthreads
-- Looking for pthread_create in pthreads - not found
-- Looking for pthread_create in pthread
-- Looking for pthread_create in pthread - found
-- Found Threads: TRUE
-- Check if compiler accepts -pthread
-- Check if compiler accepts -pthread - yes
-- Configuring done
-- Generating done
-- Build files have been written to: /home/ubuntu/wabt/build
```

Figure 3-1. *Make WABT*

Figure 3-2 shows the build process for the WABT utility.

```
root@INLN34327424A:/home/ubuntu/wabt/build# cmake --build .
Scanning dependencies of target wabt
[  1%] Building CXX object CMakeFiles/wabt.dir/src/apply-names.cc.o
[  1%] Building CXX object CMakeFiles/wabt.dir/src/binary.cc.o
[  2%] Building CXX object CMakeFiles/wabt.dir/src/binary-reader.cc.o
[  3%] Building CXX object CMakeFiles/wabt.dir/src/binary-reader-ir.cc.o
[  3%] Building CXX object CMakeFiles/wabt.dir/src/binary-reader-logging.cc.o
[  4%] Building CXX object CMakeFiles/wabt.dir/src/binary-writer.cc.o
[  4%] Building CXX object CMakeFiles/wabt.dir/src/binary-writer-spec.cc.o
[  5%] Building CXX object CMakeFiles/wabt.dir/src/binding-hash.cc.o
[  6%] Building CXX object CMakeFiles/wabt.dir/src/color.cc.o
[  6%] Building CXX object CMakeFiles/wabt.dir/src/common.cc.o
[  7%] Building CXX object CMakeFiles/wabt.dir/src/config.cc.o
[  7%] Building CXX object CMakeFiles/wabt.dir/src/decompiler.cc.o
[  8%] Building CXX object CMakeFiles/wabt.dir/src/error-formatter.cc.o
[  9%] Building CXX object CMakeFiles/wabt.dir/src/expr-visitor.cc.o
[  9%] Building CXX object CMakeFiles/wabt.dir/src/feature.cc.o
[ 10%] Building CXX object CMakeFiles/wabt.dir/src/filenames.cc.o
[ 11%] Building CXX object CMakeFiles/wabt.dir/src/generate-names.cc.o
[ 11%] Building CXX object CMakeFiles/wabt.dir/src/hash-util.cc.o
[ 12%] Building CXX object CMakeFiles/wabt.dir/src/ir.cc.o
[ 12%] Building CXX object CMakeFiles/wabt.dir/src/ir-util.cc.o
[ 13%] Building CXX object CMakeFiles/wabt.dir/src/leb128.cc.o
[ 14%] Building CXX object CMakeFiles/wabt.dir/src/lexer-source.cc.o
[ 14%] Building CXX object CMakeFiles/wabt.dir/src/lexer-source-line-finder.cc.o
[ 15%] Building CXX object CMakeFiles/wabt.dir/src/literal.cc.o
[ 15%] Building CXX object CMakeFiles/wabt.dir/src/opcode.cc.o
[ 16%] Building C object CMakeFiles/wabt.dir/src/opcode-code-table.c.o
[ 17%] Building CXX object CMakeFiles/wabt.dir/src/option-parser.cc.o
[ 17%] Building CXX object CMakeFiles/wabt.dir/src/resolve-names.cc.o
[ 18%] Building CXX object CMakeFiles/wabt.dir/src/shared-validator.cc.o
[ 19%] Building CXX object CMakeFiles/wabt.dir/src/stream.cc.o
[ 19%] Building CXX object CMakeFiles/wabt.dir/src/string-view.cc.o
[ 20%] Building CXX object CMakeFiles/wabt.dir/src/token.cc.o
[ 20%] Building CXX object CMakeFiles/wabt.dir/src/tracing.cc.o
```

Figure 3-2. *Building WABT*

Once you have built and installed the toolkit, you see the different executables like wat2wasm and wasm2wat under the bin directory. Now let's walk through a simple example of creating a wat file by hand. You can open any text editor like TextPad++ and create an example.wat file.

```
root@INLN34327424A:/home/ubuntu/wabt# cd ..
Create a directory named wat
root@INLN34327424A:/home/ubuntu# mkdir wat
```

```
root@INLN34327424A:/home/ubuntu# cd wat
Create an example.wat file
root@INLN34327424A:/home/ubuntu/wat# nano example.wat
```

Copy the following content. (I explain it a bit later.)

```
(module
  (func (result i32)
    (i32.const 100)
  )
  (export "hellowat2wasm" (func 0))
)
```

A wat file starts with the declaration of a module.

```
(module)
```

The next step is to define a function with the following signature.

```
(func <parameters/result> <local variables> <function body>)
```

It starts with the func keyword followed by parameters it accepts or the return type.

Wasm supports only numeric types, so the parameters are as follows.

- i32: a 32-bit integer

- i64: a 64-bit integer

- f32: a 32-bit float

- f64: a 64-bit float

The params for the functions are written as follows.

```
(param i32)
(param i64)
(param f32)
(param f64)
```

The result is written as follows.

```
(result i32)
(result i64)
(result f32)
(result f64)
```

In this example, you see a definition of the function with a i32 (32-bit integer) return type.

The next part of the function definition is the function body. Here the expression is i32.const 100. This expression pushes the value 100 onto the stack. (Recall from Chapter 1 that WebAssembly is a stack-based architecture.)

The last step is the export of the defined function. The export step is crucial because it makes the function visible to the host. The guest module exposes the function with index 0 (this module only defines one function) to the host runtime (Node.js in this case).

Name the hellowat2wasm function, which the host uses when invoking the function within the Wasm module.

Since there is a high-level understanding of the text format of the Wasm module, it's time to create a Wasm module from the wat file. Let's execute the wat2wasm executable (built as part of the cmake utilities you ran) and pass example.wat as input.

```
root@INLN34327424A:/home/ubuntu/wat# ../wabt/bin/wat2wasm
example.wat
```

You see the generated Wasm file called example.wasm.

```
root@INLN34327424A:/home/ubuntu/wat# ls
example.wasm  example.wat
```

Time for loading and execution of the Wasm file.

Let's use a Node.js-based runtime to load the Wasm file. Please make sure you have Node.js installed on the machine.

Create an index.js file in the wat directory.

Copy the following content into the file and save it.

```
const { readFileSync } = require("fs");

const run = async () => {
  const buffer = readFileSync("./example.wasm");
  const module = await WebAssembly.compile(buffer);
  const instance = await WebAssembly.instantiate(module);
  console.log(instance.exports.hellowat2wasm());
};

run();
```

In this code, you load the example.wasm file into a memory buffer and then instantiate the module. Once you have instantiated the module, invoke the hellowat2wasm function, which was exported by the Wasm module.

Execute the program using the following command.

```
node index.js
```

You should see 100 as the output.

Let's proceed to a little more advanced wat program, where you create a wat file to add two integers.

Again, start with the module.

```
(module
```

Next, define the function signature. Here you can see that for parameters, $a and $b are the variable names, and a 32-bit integer is returned as a result.

```
(func (param $a i32) (param $b i32) (result i32)
```

The function body, get_local $a and get_local $b, pushes the a and b values on the stack.

```
get_local $a
get_local $b
```

The i32.add pops the two values from the stack and adds them, and pushes the result back on the stack.

```
i32.add
)
```

Finally, it's time to export the add function to the host runtime.

```
(export "add" (func 0))
)
```

The following is the complete code.

```
(module
(func (param $a i32) (param $b i32) (result i32)
    get_local $a
    get_local $b
    i32.add
)
  (export "add" (func 0))
)
```

Next, use the wat2wasm tool to generate the add.wasm file.

Now it is time to consume this Wasm module from the Node.js runtime.

Create an add.js file.

Copy the following code into the file.

```
const { readFileSync } = require("fs");

const run = async () => {
  const buffer = readFileSync("./add.wasm");
  const module = await WebAssembly.compile(buffer);
  const instance = await WebAssembly.instantiate(module);
  console.log(instance.exports.add(34,76));
};

run();
```

The code loaded the add.wasm file into the memory buffer, created an instance, and invoked the add method on the exported Wasm module.

If all goes well, you should see 110 being printed on the console.

Now let's build a small calculator using the wat file, which defines three functions and exposes all three functions to the host.

The calc.wat file is defined as follows.

```
(module
//Define the first function for addition as was done in
previous example
(func (param $a i32) (param $b i32) (result i32)
    get_local $a
    get_local $b
    i32.add
)
```

Define the second function for the subtraction of the two numbers. The local variables are pushed to the stack, and i32.sub then pops the value from the stack, subtracts the two, and pushes the result again.

```
(func (param $a i32) (param $b i32) (result i32)
    get_local $a
    get_local $b
    i32.sub
)
```

Define the third function for multiplication. The i32.mul instruction pops the two values from the stack, multiplies them, and pushes the result back to the stack.

```
(func (param $a i32) (param $b i32) (result i32)
    get_local $a
    get_local $b
    i32.mul
)
  (export "add" (func 0))
  (export "subtract" (func 1))
  (export "multiply" (func 2))
)
```

Now use the wat2wasm tool to generate the Wasm file from the calc. wat file.

Once this is done, you create a simple Node.js program.

```
const { readFileSync } = require("fs");

const run = async () => {
  const buffer = readFileSync("./calc.wasm");
  const module = await WebAssembly.compile(buffer);
  const instance = await WebAssembly.instantiate(module);
var sum=  instance.exports.add(34,76);
var diff=instance.exports.subtract(76,34);
var mul=instance.exports.multiply(12,8);
console.log("sum of 34 and 76="+sum);
console.log("difference of 76 and 34="+diff);
console.log("product of 12 and 8="+mul);
};

run();
```

This program loads the calc.wasm file and invokes the exported functions one by one.

So far, you have seen how to create a wat file that exported three functions, which the host runtime can then consume. Next, let's dig a bit more deeply into the WebAssembly text format, where you see how one function in a module can invoke another function in the same module.

Let's start by defining a simple wat file with an addition function.

```
(module
(func (param $a i32) (param $b i32) (result i32)
    get_local $a
    get_local $b
    i32.add
)
  (export "add" (func 0))
)
```

You already know this function. Next, let's create a wrapper around this function.

Create a file called wrap.wat.

Copy the following code into the file.

```
(module
(func  (param $a i32) (param $b i32) (result i32)
    get_local $a
    get_local $b
    i32.add
)
```

```
(func (result i32)
    i32.const 56
    i32.const 44
    call 0
)

  (export "add1" (func 1))
)
```

The preceding code defines an add function, which gets two integers from the stack, adds them, and pushes the result onto the stack. Next, wrap the function with another function, where you put 56 and 44 onto the stack and then call the wrapped add function. Finally, expose this wrapper as add1 to the host.

Next, create a Node.js file wrap.js and copy the following code into it.

```
const { readFileSync } = require("fs");

const run = async () => {
  const buffer = readFileSync("./wrap.wasm");
  const module = await WebAssembly.compile(buffer);
  const instance = await WebAssembly.instantiate(module);
  console.log(instance.exports.add1());
};

run();
```

You can see the add1 function is invoked, which prints the result as 100.

So far, you have seen how to consume an exported function from a Wasm module and how the Node.js runtime consumes it. Next, let's import a function from the Node.js host and invoke it within the Wasm module.

Let's define an add function at the host runtime (Node.js) and then invoke it via a function defined in the Wasm module. Create an export.wat file and copy the following code into the file.

```
(module
  (import "example" "add" (func $add (param i32) (param i32)))
  (func (export "add1")
    i32.const 56
    i32.const 44

    call $add))
```

The preceding code creates a Wasm module with an exported add1 function. This function puts two values (56 and 44) on the stack and makes a call to an add function, which, in turn, invokes the add function defined on the host under the namespace example. The import statement here is telling to import add function from an example namespace. Instead of calling $add, you can also invoke the add function by call 0 instruction as 0 is the index of the add function.

Generate the Wasm file (export.wasm) using the wat2wasm utility before using it in the JavaScript file.

```
const { readFileSync } = require("fs");

const run = async () => {
var importObject = {
  example: {
    add: function(arg1,arg2) {
      sum=arg1+arg2;
        console.log("sum="+sum);
    }
  }
};
  const buffer = readFileSync("./export.wasm");
  const module = await WebAssembly.compile(buffer);
```

```
  const instance = await WebAssembly.instantiate(module,
  importObject);
  instance.exports.add1();
};

run();
```

Let's now explore WebAssembly memory. It is important to know how to isolate Wasm modules and deal with types other than integer and floats. As you know, Wasm only allows four basic types (i32, i64, f32, and f64) to be passed between the host and guest.

Knowledge of the Wasm memory model allows you to encode complex types between host and guest. You see some examples of this in later chapters.

In WebAssembly, memory is a linear array of bytes that can grow over time. WebAssembly provides instructions like i32.load and i32.store to read and write from the specific memory area. The host creates this linear memory array and provides it to the Wasm module. The Wasm module code only has visibility within that memory area, and it remains isolated from other modules running on the same host. This is how Wasm achieves memory sandboxing.

If the host is a JavaScript-based Node.js, think of this linear memory as an ArrayBuffer. To encode complex types like the string, you need to represent/encode this string into a byte array within the memory allocated for the Wasm module.

Here, a Wasm module is defined using the wat file. Create a string.wat file and copy the following content into that file.

```
(module
  (import "example" "log" (func $log (param i32 i32)))
  (import "js" "mem" (memory 1))
  (data (i32.const 0) "Hello Wat")
  (func (export "logme")
```

```
i32.const 0   ;; pass offset 0 to log
i32.const 9   ;; pass length 9 to log
call $log))
```

Import one function and one variable from the runtime host. The function is the example namespaced log function, and the variable is the JavaScript namespaced mem variable. The idea here is that you create a string in Wasm memory (a linear memory provisioned by the host) from the guest and then pass the offset and length to the host. The host can then read from that offset to the length and then decode the string and print it.

Define a data segment in the wat file, and its content is "Hello Wat". The data segment allows you to write a string into the Wasm memory at a given offset. A logme function exports two constants (offset and length) onto the stack and invokes the log function internally. This log function passes the offset and length to the host, which reads from the Wasm module memory at the offset until the length and prints the content.

Convert the string.wat file to a string.wasm file using the wat2wasm tool.

The following is the JavaScript code for defining the imports and invoking the logme function on the Wasm module.

```
const { readFileSync } = require("fs");
// this is one of the variable which will be imported by the guest
var memory = new WebAssembly.Memory({ initial : 1 });
const run = async () => {
var importObject = {
//the function and memory are defined as imports .These are
imported by the Wasm module.
  example: {
    log: function(offset,length) {
var bytes = new Uint8Array(memory.buffer, offset, length);
```

```
    var string = new TextDecoder('utf8').decode(bytes);
    console.log(string);
      }
    }
,js: {
          mem: memory
        }
};
  const buffer = readFileSync("./string.wasm");
  const module = await WebAssembly.compile(buffer);
  const instance = await WebAssembly.instantiate(module,
                    importObject);
  instance.exports.logme();
};
run();
```

The JavaScript file, when executed within Node.js, should print Hello Wat on the console. This file defines two imports.

- The example.log function reads the memory array at a specific offset and to a specific length. Offset and length are provided by the guest, which has put the "Hello Wat" string into that array.

- The memory array itself.

The host's job is to pass this memory to the guest. This is done via importObject, which is imported into the Wasm module. The Wasm module puts the string into the memory and passes the offset and length of the memory the host has allocated it. The guest invokes the example.log function on the host. This function reads the memory at offset and length and prints the contents.

This is how you can achieve communication between the host and the guest.

Tables

Let's look at the tables section in the wat file. You know that functions within a module can only be invoked by passing the function's index to the call instruction. An instruction called call_indirect in Wasm provides a layer of indirection to the function calls. With the call instruction, the index passed is the index of the exact location of the function in memory, where call_indirect allows to invoke the function by an indirection by a structure called a table. The table holds the actual function location and maps this index to a virtual index used by the host code. This allows you to do late binding to the function call; for example, hosts that are compiled. For example, a Rust binary can decide at runtime which function to call by passing the index of the function to be invoked. This is a powerful mechanism provided by WebAssembly for the dynamic runtime invocation of a function.

Let's look at a wat file.

Create a table.wat file and copy the following code.

```
(module
  (table 3 funcref)
(func $f1 (param $a i32) (param $b i32) (result i32)
    get_local $a
    get_local $b
    i32.add
)
(func $f2 (param $a i32) (param $b i32) (result i32)
    get_local $a
    get_local $b
    i32.sub
)
```

```
(func $f3 (param $a i32) (param $b i32) (result i32)
   get_local $a
   get_local $b
   i32.mul
)

   (elem (i32.const 0) $f1 $f2 $f3)
// this refers to the index of the function in the function table
   (type $return_i32 (func (param i32 i32)(result i32)))
   (func (export "callByIndex") (param  i32 i32 i32)(result i32)
local.get 1
local.get 2
local.get 0
     call_indirect (type $return_i32)
)
)
```

In the wat file, you added (table 3 funcref) just below the module
section. This tells the Wasm host to create a module of table size of 3. Here,
funcref specifies that elements of this table are references to the functions.

The add, subtract, and multiply functions are defined as usual.
The next section in the wat file is the elem, which defines the functions
referenced by the table. In our case, the add, subtract, and multiply
functions are part of the elem section.

The (type $return_i32 (func (param i32 i32)(result i32))) section
specifies the type of the function to be invoked. In this case, since all three
functions have similar signatures, you keep one type.

Finally, the following segment exports the callByIndex function to the
host.

```
   (func (export "callByIndex") (param  i32 i32 i32)(result i32)
local.get 1
local.get 2
```

```
local.get 0
  call_indirect (type $return_i32)
```

This function takes three integer parameters. The first is the index of the function in the table. The other two are the parameters to be operated upon by the function to be invoked, like add, multiply, or subtract.

local.get 1, local.get 2, and local.get 0 push the index of the function and two other values on the stack. By default, the call_indirect instruction pops the top value from the stack. Because you push the function's index on the stack, it picks up, and the actual function is invoked. The callee then pops the other two values from the stack and invokes the needed operation.

Create a Wasm file from the wat file using the wat2wasm utility.

Now let's invoke the module function by index in the following JavaScript code.

```
const { readFileSync } = require("fs");

const run = async () => {
  const buffer = readFileSync("./table.wasm");
  const module = await WebAssembly.compile(buffer);
  const instance = await WebAssembly.instantiate(module);
var sum=  instance.exports.callByIndex(0,56,34);
var diff=instance.exports.callByIndex(1,56,34);
var mul=instance.exports.callByIndex(2,12,8);
console.log("sum of 34 and 56="+sum);
console.log("difference of 56 and 34="+diff);
console.log("product of 12 and 8="+mul);
};
run();
```

You can see how the individual functions are invoked using a specific index in a Wasm module table. You can take this index as input or based on some logic and dynamically call a function.

These tables can also be dynamically created by the host and can also be shared between different modules. However, this kind of dynamic linking is beyond the scope of this book.

The wasm2wat Utility

Now that you've seen the wat2wasm tool, let's look at a tool that reverses the process, which means taking a Wasm file and generating a wat file. This can help debug a Wasm file.

Take the calc.wasm file generated in the previous section and use the wasm2wat executable against it. The wasm2wat executable is located in the same location as the wat2wasm binary (under the wabt/bin directory).

Run the following command.

```
../wabt/bin/wasm2wat calc.wasm -o calc1.wat
```

Next, let's provide calc.wasm as input and calc1.wat as output. Inspect the calc1.wat file, as follows.

```
(module
  (type (;0;) (func (param i32 i32) (result i32)))
  (func (;0;) (type 0) (param i32 i32) (result i32)
    local.get 0
    local.get 1
    i32.add)
  (func (;1;) (type 0) (param i32 i32) (result i32)
    local.get 0
    local.get 1
    i32.sub)
  (func (;2;) (type 0) (param i32 i32) (result i32)
```

```
    local.get 0
    local.get 1
    i32.mul)
  (export "add" (func 0))
  (export "subtract" (func 1))
  (export "multiply" (func 2)))
```

This tool can help one to debug and look at some possible issues in the Wasm file.

Object Dump Using wasm-objdump

wasm-objdump is a utility that allows you to do a dump of the WebAssembly file. It prints information about the Wasm binary file. You can pass flags to print different details, like headers, full content, and function bodies.

The below prints the header information for the add.wasm file.

```
ubuntu@INLN34327424A:~/wat$ sudo ../wabt/bin/wasm-objdump add.
wasm -h
```

```
add.wasm:          file format wasm 0x1
```

The following are the sections.

```
    Type start=0x0000000a end=0x00000011 (size=0x00000007)
    count: 1
 Function start=0x00000013 end=0x00000015 (size=0x00000002)
count: 1
   Export start=0x00000017 end=0x0000001e (size=0x00000007)
   count: 1
     Code start=0x00000020 end=0x00000029 (size=0x00000009)
     count: 1
```

Passing the disassemble flag (-d) results in the following output.

```
ubuntu@INLN34327424A:~/wat$ sudo ../wabt/bin/wasm-objdump add.
wasm -d
```

```
add.wasm:       file format wasm 0x1
```

The following shows the code disassembly.

```
000022 func[0] <add>:
 000023: 20 00                          | local.get 0
 000025: 20 01                          | local.get 1
 000027: 6a                             | i32.add
 000028: 0b                             | end
```

Run the following command (-x as the flag) to get the section information.

```
ubuntu@INLN34327424A:~/wat$ sudo ../wabt/bin/wasm-objdump add.
wasm -x
```

```
add.wasm:       file format wasm 0x1
```

These are the section details.

```
Type[1]:
 - type[0] (i32, i32) -> i32
Function[1]:
 - func[0] sig=0 <add>
Export[1]:
 - func[0] <add> -> "add"
Code[1]:
 - func[0] size=7 <add>
```

Apart from the utilities, there are more utilities like wasm-interp, wasm-decompile, and wasm-strip. These are left for you to experiment with.

Summary

This chapter discussed utilities like wat2wasm, where you wrote the wat files by hand and learned their segments and structure. You also saw how functions could be exported and imported using the wat format. The chapter also covered other utilities like wasm2wat and utilities for generating the dump of the Wasm file.

CHAPTER 4

WebAssembly with Rust and JavaScript: An Introduction to wasm-bindgen

This chapter discusses how WebAssembly-based modules can be invoked by the runtime host and vice versa.

WebAssembly allows only numeric data types (integer and float) to pass between the host and the Wasm module. Since most of the functionality of programs depends on complex types like strings and other custom data types, a programmer must encode and decode these integers/floats into the specific data type.

Fortunately for languages like Rust, Mozilla has provided a toolchain called wasm-bindgen, which generates this glue coding. The glue code does the heavy lifting of generating the needed stubs and skeletons needed both on the host and the Wasm side to encode the specific data type into integer and then decode the same from integer array to the specific data type. Much of this chapter is devoted to this tool called wasm-bindgen.

© Shashank Mohan Jain 2022
S. M. Jain, *WebAssembly for Cloud*, https://doi.org/10.1007/978-1-4842-7496-5_4

wasm-bindgen

wasm-bindgen provides a channel between JavaScript and WebAssembly to communicate something other than numbers (i.e., objects, strings, arrays, custom types). The wasm-bindgen tool allows Rust to see JavaScript classes, expose and invoke callbacks in either language, send strings as function parameters, and return complex values. The same applies to JavaScript; it allows JavaScript to use Rust functions and structures and invoke callbacks. This makes the two languages work so smoothly together that it does not seem that they are different.

At the basic level, wasm-bindgen injects some metadata into your compiled WebAssembly module. Then, a separate command-line tool reads that metadata to generate an appropriate JavaScript wrapper containing the functions, classes, and other primitives that the developer wants to be bound to Rust.

Let's look at a simple example of wasm-bindgen.

Prerequisites

Let's assume that Rust is set up on a Linux machine. All the examples in this chapter used Rust version 1.54.0. If not, you can set it up using the instructions at www.rust-lang.org/tools/install.

Also, make sure that npm and node are installed (npm version 7.20.3 and node version 7.20.3 were used in this chapter).

Next, you need to install wasm-bindgen.

```
cargo install wasm-bindgen-cli
```

The dependent crates are downloaded and installed (see Figure 4-1).

```
Updating crates.io index
Downloaded wasm-bindgen-cli v0.2.74
Downloaded 1 crate (42.0 KB) in 11.73s
Installing wasm-bindgen-cli v0.2.74
Downloaded form_urlencoded v1.0.1
Downloaded pkg-config v0.3.19
Downloaded chrono v0.4.19
Downloaded matches v0.1.8
Downloaded standback v0.2.17
Downloaded wit-schema-version v0.1.0
Downloaded time v0.1.43
Downloaded strsim v0.10.0
Downloaded mime_guess v2.0.3
Downloaded wit text v0.8.0
Downloaded chunked_transfer v1.4.0
Downloaded idna v0.2.3
Downloaded url v2.2.2
Downloaded safemem v0.3.3
Downloaded remove_dir_all v0.5.3
Downloaded unicase v2.6.0
Downloaded tempfile v3.2.0
Downloaded threadpool v1.8.1
Downloaded socket2 v0.4.1
Downloaded unicode-bidi v0.3.5
Downloaded wast v21.0.0
Downloaded tiny_http v0.8.2
Downloaded wit-validator v0.2.1
Downloaded sha1 v0.6.0
Downloaded wit-writer v0.2.0
Downloaded wit-parser v0.2.0
Downloaded walrus-macro v0.19.0
Downloaded time-macros-impl v0.1.2
Downloaded wasm-bindgen-multi-value-xform v0.2.74
Downloaded wasm-bindgen-externref-xform v0.2.74
Downloaded filetime v0.2.14
Downloaded wit-walrus v0.6.0
Downloaded wasm-bindgen-threads-xform v0.2.74
Downloaded time v0.2.27
Downloaded wasmparser v0.77.0
Downloaded wasm-bindgen-wasm-interpreter v0.2.74
Downloaded buf_redux v0.8.4
Downloaded wasmparser v0.59.0
Downloaded twoway v0.1.8
Downloaded base64 v0.9.3
Downloaded curl v0.4.38
Downloaded ascii v1.0.0
```

Figure 4-1. *Building the Rust project in progress*

If the build fails with SSL errors, try installing pkg-config using

```
apt install pkg-config
apt-get install libssl-dev
```

Once the wasm-bindgen CLI is installed, create a simple project in Rust using the cargo package manager.

```
ubuntu@INLN34327424A:~/shashank$ cargo new sample_binding_
demo -lib (there is a double hyphen before lib)
```

You get the following output.

```
Created library `sample_binding_demo` package
Change directory sample_binding_demo
```

There is a file called Cargo.toml.

```
[package]
name = "sample_binding_demo"
version = "0.1.0"
edition = "2018"
```

More keys and their definitions are at `https://doc.rust-lang.org/cargo/reference/manifest.html`.

```
[dependencies]
```

In the Cargo.toml file, the dependencies are blank. When using wasm-bindgen, you need to make this as a dependency in the dependencies section. You also need to add crate-type = ["cdylib"] under the lib section of the Cargo.toml file. This option allows you to generate a dynamic library, such as a SO file for Linux or a DLL file for Windows, but when the compiler target is wasm32-unknown-unknown, it generates a Wasm file. A wasm32-unknown-unknown target compiles Rust to the WebAssembly module.

Changed cargo.toml file

```
[package]
name = "sample_binding_demo"
version = "0.1.0"
edition = "2018"
```

More keys and their definitions are at https://doc.rust-lang.org/
cargo/reference/manifest.html.

[lib]
crate-type = ["cdylib"]

```
[dependencies]
```
wasm-bindgen = "0.2"

Save the changes.

Now go to the src directory and open the lib.rs file.

Add the following lines of code (i.e., replace all the lib.rs content with this content).

```
extern crate wasm_bindgen;
use wasm_bindgen::prelude::*;

#[wasm_bindgen]
extern "C" {
    fn alert(s: &str);
}

// Export a 'greetMe' function
#[wasm_bindgen]
pub fn greetMe(name: &str) {
    alert(&format!("Greetings, {}!", name));
}
```

The preceding code exports the greetMe function from the Wasm module to the host. Internally this greetMe function calls an alert function on the host side. The host side is assumed to be a JavaScript engine, and its alert function is invoked. The preceding example demonstrates how a host (JavaScript runtime like Node.js) can invoke a Rust function by passing a string parameter to it. Then the Wasm module (Rust-based) invokes a JavaScript function (alert function) back on the host.

The catch here is that Wasm doesn't support the passing of strings or complex types. There must be some glue coding that needs to do this encoding and decoding for us. This is what wasm-bindgen provides.

Next, let's compile the code and generate the necessary stubs.

Before building the code, you need to add the Wasm compilation target using the following command.

```
rustup target add wasm32-unknown-unknown
```

Run the command to generate the Wasm file.

```
ubuntu@INLN34327424A:~/shashank/sample_binding_demo$ cargo
build --target wasm32-unknown-unknown
```

By listing the build artifacts, you can see the sample_binding_demo. wasm file in the following directory.

```
ubuntu@INLN34327424A:~/shashank/sample_binding_demo$ ll
target/wasm32-unknown-unknown/debug/
build/          .cargo-lock    deps/              examples/
.fingerprint/   incremental/   sample_binding_demo.d
sample_binding_demo.wasm
```

1. After generating this Wasm file, you may think that this is enough, but you need to do a bit more before you are ready to load and invoke this WebAssembly file.

The wasm-bindgen CLI modifies Wasm files and generates the necessary glue code on the host (JavaScript) side.

Run the following command.

```
ubuntu@INLN34327424A:~/shashank/sample_binding_demo$ wasm-
bindgen target/wasm32-unknown-unknown/debug/sample_binding_
demo.wasm --out-dir .
```

After listing the files in the current directory, you see some new files.

```
ubuntu@INLN34327424A:~/shashank/sample_binding_demo$ ls
Cargo.lock  Cargo.toml  sample_binding_demo_bg.js  sample_
binding_demo_bg.wasm  sample_binding_demo_bg.wasm.d.ts  sample_
binding_demo.d.ts  sample_binding_demo.js  src  target
```

Out of these files, sample_binding_demo_bg.js is relevant. The file looks like the following.

```
import * as wasm from './sample_binding_demo_bg.wasm';

const lTextDecoder = typeof TextDecoder === 'undefined' ?
(0, module.require)('util').TextDecoder : TextDecoder;

let cachedTextDecoder = new lTextDecoder('utf-8', { ignoreBOM:
true, fatal: true });
```

Line 1 imports the generated a Wasm module.

Lines 2 and 3 define the TextDecoder. TextDecoder is used to decode the integers back to a string.

Within the code, the encoder is defined as follows.

```
const lTextEncoder = typeof TextEncoder === 'undefined' ?
(0, module.require)('util').TextEncoder : TextEncoder;

let cachedTextEncoder = new lTextEncoder('utf-8');
```

The following is an important function defined in the sample_binding_demo_bg.js file.

```
function getStringFromWasm0(ptr, len) {
    return cachedTextDecoder.decode(getUint8Memory0().
    subarray(ptr, ptr + len));
}
```

This function takes two inputs.

- ptr is the pointer to the memory location within the Wasm module.

- len is the length, which is read starting from the ptr location.

The module populates these memory locations with the integer data (e.g., the greeting string is represented by integers). The function then decodes the array of integers back to the string.

The following is another important function defined in the sample_binding_demo_bg.js file.

```
function passStringToWasm0(arg, malloc, realloc) {

    if (realloc === undefined) {
        const buf = cachedTextEncoder.encode(arg);
        const ptr = malloc(buf.length);
        getUint8Memory0().subarray(ptr, ptr + buf.length).
        set(buf);
        WASM_VECTOR_LEN = buf.length;
        return ptr;
    }

    let len = arg.length;
    let ptr = malloc(len);
```

```
const mem = getUint8Memory0();

let offset = 0;

for (; offset < len; offset++) {
    const code = arg.charCodeAt(offset);
    if (code > 0x7F) break;
    mem[ptr + offset] = code;
}

if (offset !== len) {
    if (offset !== 0) {
        arg = arg.slice(offset);
    }
    ptr = realloc(ptr, len, len = offset + arg.length * 3);
    const view = getUint8Memory0().subarray(ptr + offset,
    ptr + len);
const ret = encodeString(arg, view);

    offset += ret.written;
}

WASM_VECTOR_LEN = offset;
return ptr;
}
```

The passStringToWasm0 function creates the memory within the
Wasm module and then encoding the string as an array of integers into
the memory. It returns the pointer to the start of the string. The WASM_
VECTOR_LEN variable represents the offset, which the string represents in
the array.

The following is the third important function in the sample_binding_
demo_bg.js file.

```
export function greetMe(name) {
    var ptr0 = passStringToWasm0(name, wasm.__wbindgen_malloc,
    wasm.__wbindgen_realloc);
    var len0 = WASM_VECTOR_LEN;
    wasm.greetMe(ptr0, len0);
}
```

Line 2 of this function calls the passStringToWasm0 function, which
returns the pointer to the start of the array. This encodes the passed name
second variable is the length of the string (offset).

Finally, call the wasm.greetMe function passing the pointer and offset.

The preceding are the generated JavaScript files and functions on the
host side. The wasm-bindgen tool also modifies the Wasm file to make it
compatible with the JavaScript host.

Now, let's look at how this function is defined in the modified Wasm
file.

First, you need to have the WABT tools installed. On Ubuntu, it can be
installed using the following command.

```
sudo apt-get install wabt
```

Or it can be installed following the instructions from https://github.
com/WebAssembly/wabt.

```
ubuntu@INLN34327424A:~/shashank$ wabt/bin/wasm2wat sample_
binding_demo/sample_binding_demo_bg.wasm | grep greet
```

```
(func $sample_binding_demo::greetMe::h0099f4e1d51123d4 (type 5)
(param i32 i32)
  (func $greetMe (type 5) (param i32 i32)
    call $sample_binding_demo::greetMe::h0099f4e1d51123d4
  (export "greetMe" (func $greetMe))
```

66

The function takes two integers as input (pointer and offset). Within the generated Wasm file, the function describes how it is defined in the Wasm bytecode format.

```
(func $sample_binding_demo::greetMe::h0099f4e1d51123d4 (type 5)
(param i32 i32)
    (local i32 i32 i32 i32 i32 i32 i32 i32 i32 i32 i32 i32 i32
i32 i32 i32 i32 i32 i32 i32 i32 i32 i32 i32 i32 i32 i32 i32 i32
i32 i32 i32 i32 i32 i32 i32 i32 i32 i32 i32 i32 i32 i32 i32 i32
i32 i32 i64)
    global.get 0
    local.set 2
    i32.const 96
    local.set 3
    local.get 2
    local.get 3
    i32.sub
    local.set 4
    local.get 4
    global.set 0
    local.get 4
    local.get 0
    i32.store offset=16
```

. . . .

So far, you've seen that via the wasm-bindgen tool, you can generate the JavaScript stubs for the host to encode the types like string into an array of integers that the Wasm module can consume. Similarly, you also saw that wasm-bindgen generates a decoder glue logic for converting back the array of an integer into the desired type (in this case, a string).

Now you create an index.js file (it should be in the same location the wasm-bindgen tool generated the stub files), which invokes the stub, and through it, the Wasm module.

```
const wasm = import('./sample_binding_demo');
wasm
    .then(m => m.greetMe("Shashank"))
    .catch(console.error);
```

The sample_binding_demo JavaScript file imports the Wasm file and the JavaScript file, which interface with the Wasm module.

```
import * as wasm from "./sample_binding_demo_bg.wasm";
export * from "./sample_binding_demo_bg.js";
```

webpack is used for this demo.

Install webpack using npm using the following commands.

```
npm i webpack
npm i webpack-dev-server
```

Now create a webpack.config.js file as follows.

```
const path = require('path');
const HtmlWebpackPlugin = require('html-webpack-plugin');
const webpack = require('webpack');

module.exports = {
    entry: './index.js',
    output: {
        path: path.resolve(__dirname, 'dist'),
        filename: 'index.js',
    },

    plugins: [
        new HtmlWebpackPlugin(),
        new webpack.ProvidePlugin({
```

```
            TextDecoder: ['text-encoding', 'TextDecoder'],
            TextEncoder: ['text-encoding', 'TextEncoder']
        })
    ],

    mode: 'development'
};
```

Next, create a package.json file.

```
{

    "scripts": {
    "build": "webpack",
    "http_server": "webpack-dev-server"
    },

    "devDependencies": {
        "text-encoding": "^0.7.0",
        "html-webpack-plugin": "^3.2.0",
        "webpack": "^4.11.1",
        "webpack-cli": "^3.1.1",
        "webpack-dev-server": "^3.1.0"
    }
}
```

Let's now launch the HTTP server using the following command.

```
npm run http_server
```

You can now access the webpage in the browser.

Figure 4-2 shows a simple example of using wasm-bindgen to expose Rust code back to JavaScript and vice versa.

```
ubuntu@INLN34327424A:~/shashank/bindgen_demo$ npm run http_server

> http_server
> webpack-dev-server --host 0.0.0.0 --port 9000 --disable-host-check --useLocalIp

ℹ ｢wds｣: Project is running at http://172.20.10.10:9000/
ℹ ｢wds｣: webpack output is served from /
ℹ ｢wds｣: Content not from webpack is served from /home/ubuntu/shashank/bindgen_demo
ℹ ｢wdm｣: Hash: fad59b950026cfadaecf
Version: webpack 4.46.0
Time: 1879ms
Built at: 07/16/2021 12:49:29 PM
                       Asset      Size  Chunks                    Chunk Names
                    0.index.js  623 KiB       0  [emitted]
                    1.index.js  6.34 KiB      1  [emitted]
b97813b2bea19ad2cac7.module.wasm  65.9 KiB    1  [emitted] [immutable]
                    index.html  181 bytes        [emitted]
                      index.js  376 KiB    main  [emitted]            main
Entrypoint main = index.js
[0] multi (webpack)-dev-server/client?http://172.20.10.10:9000 ./index.js 40 bytes {main} [built]
[./bindgen_demo.js] 85 bytes {1} [built]
[./bindgen_demo_bg.js] 2.5 KiB {1} [built]
[./bindgen_demo_bg.wasm] 65.9 KiB {1} [built]
[./index.js] 105 bytes {main} [built]
[./node_modules/ansi-html/index.js] 4.16 KiB {main} [built]
[./node_modules/strip-ansi/index.js] 161 bytes {main} [built]
[./node_modules/webpack-dev-server/client/index.js?http://172.20.10.10:9000] (webpack)-dev-server/client?http://172.20.10.10:9000 4.29 KiB {main} [built]
[./node_modules/webpack-dev-server/client/overlay.js] (webpack)-dev-server/client/overlay.js 3.51 KiB {main} [built]
[./node_modules/webpack-dev-server/client/socket.js] (webpack)-dev-server/client/socket.js 1.53 KiB {main} [built]
[./node_modules/webpack-dev-server/client/utils/createSocketUrl.js] (webpack)-dev-server/client/utils/createSocketUrl.js 2.91 KiB {main} [built]
[./node_modules/webpack-dev-server/client/utils/log.js] (webpack)-dev-server/client/utils/log.js 964 bytes {main} [built]
[./node_modules/webpack-dev-server/client/utils/reloadApp.js] (webpack)-dev-server/client/utils/reloadApp.js 1.59 KiB {main} [built]
[./node_modules/webpack-dev-server/client/utils/sendMessage.js] (webpack)-dev-server/client/utils/sendMessage.js 402 bytes {main} [built]
[./node_modules/webpack/hot sync ^\.\/log$] (webpack)/hot sync nonrecursive ^\.\/log$ 170 bytes {main} [built]
    + 26 hidden modules
Child html-webpack-plugin for "index.html":
    1 asset
    Entrypoint undefined = index.html
    [./node_modules/html-webpack-plugin/lib/loader.js!./node_modules/html-webpack-plugin/default_index.ejs] 376 bytes {0} [built]
    [./node_modules/lodash/lodash.js] 531 KiB {0} [built]
    [./node_modules/webpack/buildin/global.js] (webpack)/buildin/global.js 472 bytes {0} [built]
    [./node_modules/webpack/buildin/module.js] (webpack)/buildin/module.js 497 bytes {0} [built]
ℹ ｢wdm｣: Compiled successfully.
```

Figure 4-2. *Starting the HTTP server*

Next, let's look at a more complex example to demonstrate how a complex type can be serialized and deserialized across the JavaScript and Wasm boundaries.

Complex Types via wasm-bindgen

Let's create a person type in Rust code within the example file and add two functions: one to send the person object to JavaScript and the other to receive it from JavaScript.

Please add the following dependencies in the Cargo.toml file.

```
serde = { version = "1.0", features = ["derive"] }
wasm-bindgen = { version = "0.2", features =
["serde-serialize"] }
```

Code
```
extern crate wasm_bindgen;
```

```rust
use wasm_bindgen::prelude::*;
use std::collections::HashMap;
use serde::{Serialize, Deserialize};

#[derive(Serialize, Deserialize)]
pub struct Person {
    pub field1: HashMap<u32, String>,
    pub field2: Vec<Vec<f32>>,
    pub field3: String,
}

#[wasm_bindgen]
extern "C" {
    fn alert(s: &str);
}

// Export a 'hello' function
#[wasm_bindgen]
pub fn hello(name: &str) {
    alert(&format!("Hello, {}!", name));
}

#[wasm_bindgen]
pub fn send_person_to_js() -> JsValue {
    let mut field1 = HashMap::new();
    field1.insert(0, String::from("ex"));
    let person = Person {
        field1,
        field2: vec![vec![1., 2.], vec![3., 4.]],
        field3: "shashank".to_string()
    };

    JsValue::from_serde(&person).unwrap()
}
```

```
#[wasm_bindgen]
pub fn receive_person_from_js(val: &JsValue) {
    let _example: Person = val.into_serde().unwrap();

}
```

The definitions of type looks like this

```
#[derive(Serialize, Deserialize)]
pub struct Person {
    pub field1: HashMap<u32, String>,
    pub field2: Vec<Vec<f32>>,
    pub field3: String,
}
```

The serialize and deserialize annotation allows this type to be serializable and deserializable.

You can build the needed artifacts using the following commands.

```
Build the wasm using command below
cargo build --target wasm32-unknown-unknown
Generate the stubs using wasm bindgen using command below
wasm-bindgen target/wasm32-unknown-unknown/debug/sample_
binding_demo.wasm --out-dir .
```

This function can be invoked, similar to the example explained for string type. I leave this to you to try a specific example.

Now that you understand how to deal with types other than integers and encode complex types in WebAssembly, so it's time to move on to some real-world examples.

Let's move on to create a sample program for a Bloom filter in Rust. The goal of this chapter would be to create an example of a Bloom filter and use wasm-bindgen for generating the needed glue code for a JavaScript-based host, as well as make changes in the Wasm file using the wasm-bindgen utility.

This example is important as you take the same example throughout the book when you expand your knowledge to create a web-based interface to the Wasm module. Let's continue with the same example when you deploy the web app to Kubernetes later and see a simple HTTP interface for the same Bloom filter–based Wasm module.

Before creating the WebAssembly side, you need to understand what a Bloom filter is.

The Bloom Filter

When dealing with big data scenarios, sometimes you don't need 100% accurate results. For example, you want to count the hits to a specific webpage when the exact number is 189045; if the system tells you the number is 18900 or 189100, you can probably live with this approximation. Approximation is the main use case of probabilistic data structures. They trade some of the accuracy to save a lot of memory or storage space. A Bloom filter is one of the implementations of a probabilistic data structure.

A Bloom filter is used when you want to do a membership test. For example, you want to develop an authentication process for the large number of users in a system. Normally, the authentication system is hit each time a user logs in.

Now suppose you want to optimize this process and reject false authentication attempts before hitting the authentication system. This means you need something in memory that checks the presence of the username. However, if millions of users are in the system, storing every username in memory is not feasible for this scenario. This is where a Bloom filter comes into the picture. Instead of storing the username, you store its presence in the Bloom filter data structure.

A Bloom filter allows some false positives but don't allow false negatives. So if the Bloom filter tells a user is present, it can be a case of false positive. You can then go to the authentication system and validate

73

whether the user is a valid user or not. If the Bloom filter tells the user is not present, you can reject the call before hitting the authentication system. This can be useful in scenarios such as thwarting denial-of-service attacks on the system.

The important aspect to understand here is that the Bloom filter saves a lot of space, and you don't need to load all usernames into memory. You can roughly have millions of users' presence checked by just having a few kilobytes of memory.

How a Bloom Filter Works

A Bloom filter is a probabilistic data structure that, instead of loading actual data into memory, uses the representation of that data or, more precisely, the presence in memory.

A Bloom filter has two main components.

- An array of n bits

- Multiple hash functions which map to an index in the array

When you add an element to the Bloom filter, you hash the element using different hash functions and calculate an index in the array. A modulo operator is used to restrict the size of the index to the size of the array. For that element, whatever index is returned by the hash function(s), you mark that bit as 1 in the array.

During lookup (for example, a username), you hash the username by the different hash functions and check the bit in the different indexes returned by the hash functions. If all the bits are 1, this would mean the username is probably present (this is where false positives can creep in). But if one of the bits is 0, you can guarantee that the username is absent, thereby eliminating any false negatives.

Let's explain this using an example. Table 4-1 shows a size 10 array. All elements in the array start with 0 as the entry at each of the indices.

Table 4-1. *Bloom Filter in Its Initial State*

0	0	0	0	0	0	0	0	0	0

You need k hash functions. Let's assume $k=3$.

You also want to store a word in the Bloom filter. You need to hash the same word using all three hash functions and do a mod by 10 to get an index into the array for all three hashes.

The following is an example.

```
H1("wasm") %10 =2
H2("wasm") %10 =5
H3("wasm") %10 =3
```

The state of Bloom filter is shown in Table 4-2.

Table 4-2. *Bloom Filter After First Entries*

0	1	1	0	1	0	0	0	0	0

Let's suppose that you want to store another word, *rust*, into the Bloom filter data structure. Then, do the same operation again.

```
H1("rust") %10 =1
H2("rust") %10 =5
H3("rust") %10 =7
```

Table 4-3 shows the Bloom filter state after the second entry.

Table 4-3. *Bloom Filter After Second Entry*

1	1	1	0	1	0	1	0	0	0

Similarly, you can store representations of other words as well.

When there is a need to check for the presence of a word, this is how it works. For example, now you need to check whether the term *wasm* is present in the Bloom filter or not.

Again, do the hash operations with mod on the word (*wasm* in this case).

```
H1("wasm") %10 =2
H2("wasm") %10 =5
H3("wasm") %10 =3
```

If you check the indices in the array at 2, 5, and 3, all bits are set to 1, which means the word is present in the Bloom filter.

Take another example of search. For example, you now want to search whether the term *kube* is there as part of the Bloom filter.

Do the hash and mod on the term *kube*.

```
H1("kube") %10 =1
H2("kube") %10 =2
H3("kube") %10 =7
```

Check the array and note that all bits are set to 1 here. But wait, you never added this word to the Bloom filter. This is a classic case of a false positive, which is a possibility in a Bloom filter. You might now ask, what good is this structure? The answer is that if the Bloom filter says that the element doesn't exist, you can be certain that it's not there. If the Bloom filter says an element exists, it's possible that it does not exist.

Some of the use cases can be to maintain a list of blacklisted websites for your browser. Each blacklisted website can be encoded into the Bloom filter. Now when someone tries to visit a website, its presence is checked in the Bloom filter. If it's not found, rest assured that it is not a blacklisted website and is allowed access. If the answer is positive, it can be a false positive, which means it can still be an allowed website, but the Bloom filter has falsely classified it as a blacklisted website. This is still a fine behavior as you want a guarantee that the blacklisted websites are always blocked, and this is the guarantee you get via the Bloom filter.

The Bloom filter provides space efficiency because it's doesn't store the data but its presence. This is much more efficient than using data structures like HashMap, Tries, and so forth.

The Cuckoo Filter

A cuckoo filter is like the Bloom filter for achieving fast set membership testing.

Cuckoo filters are a data structure, described in a paper in 2014 by Fan, Andersen, Kaminsky, and Mitzenmacher. Bloom filters have a limitation that you cannot delete an entry from them.

Cuckoo filters improve upon the design of the Bloom filter by providing the following.

- Deletion

- Limited counting

- Bounded false positive probability while still maintaining a similar space complexity

Cuckoo filters under the hood use cuckoo hashing to resolve collisions and are essentially a compact cuckoo hash table. Cuckoo and Bloom filters are useful for set membership testing when the size of the original data is large. They both only use 7 bits per entry.

In our example, the idea is to create a simple cuckoo filter preloaded with certain entries. These entries are provided as JSON and loaded within the cuckoo filter. Rust is the implementation language.

Rust provides crates for a cuckoo filter. You can think of a crate as a compilation unit in Rust. The existing crates can be imported into an existing project, and their functionality can be used. Let's use a cuckoo filter crate to do the following.

- Populate it with pre-defined entries

- Provide an API to test the membership of an entry in the cuckoo filter

First, compile the Rust code to Wasm using wasm32-unknown-unknown as the compiler target, and as a next step, use wasm-bindgen to generate the stubs needed to communicate between Rust and JavaScript. The wasm-bindgen tool generates the JavaScript glue code to interface with the WebAssembly module. It modifies the existing Wasm file to allow complex data types to pass between the host (JavaScript) and the guest (Wasm module).

To test the membership of a key, pass on a key from JavaScript to the Wasm function, which in turn checks if the key is present in the cuckoo filter. This example is used throughout the book.

Cuckoo filter example

```
Create a new Rust project
Run the command
cargo new cuckoo -lib (there are two hyphens before lib)
First copy the code below into the sr/lib.rs file
// These are all the crates and libraries you need for our example
#[macro_use]
extern crate lazy_static;
extern crate wasm_bindgen;
extern crate cuckoofilter;
use wasm_bindgen::prelude::*;
use std::collections::HashMap;
```

```rust
// this library allows us to serialize and deserialize the
json. Our js code will pass json as input to wasm
//module which will deserialize it.
use serde::{Serialize, Deserialize};
// existing cuckoo filter crate
use cuckoofilter::CuckooFilter;
use std::collections::hash_map::DefaultHasher;

// lazy_static! Code snippet allows the Rust program to hold a
// global reference. Here you need to create a cuckoo filter
// Data structure as a global variable, which we will then use
// across our code. This structure is initialized at startup
// with pre existing keys
lazy_static! {

static ref cf:CuckooFilter<DefaultHasher> = {
let  CF:CuckooFilter<DefaultHasher>=load_data();
CF
};
}
// method for loading the keys. Here we have just loaded 4 but
// these entries can easily be in millions As the  goal here is
// to show a working of wasm module majorly and not Bloom
// Filter per say, we will keep the entries limited to 4.
// This method was invoked from within the lazy static method
// which then exposes a global data structure CF for the cuckoo
// filter. fn load_data() -> CuckooFilter<DefaultHasher>
{
let words = vec!["foo", "bar", "xylophone", "milagro"];
// mut keyword allows a mutable variable to be declared in Rust.
// Since you need our structure to be mutable.
```

```rust
let mut CF2:CuckooFilter<DefaultHasher> = CuckooFilter::new();

let mut insertions = 0;
// Iterate over the json entries for the keys
for s in &words {
// add them to the CF2 cuckoo filter structure
    if CF2.test_and_add(s) {
        insertions += 1;
    }
}
// we return the CuckooFilter structure from this method and this is
// referred by the CF global variable created in lazy static method.
CF2
}
// This is the crucial method with a wasm_bindgen annotation.
// This is the method exposed to the host and to the wasm bindgen
// utility to generate the glue code on js side and make
// changes on the wasm side as well. As one can see it takes
// string as input and returns a Boolean wrapped in a structure . We
// will expose the check_word_exists method to the host
//JSValue
#[wasm_bindgen]
pub fn check_word_exists(member:&str) ->JsValue
{
// check for presence of the keyword sent from host
let exists=cf.contains(member);
println!("{}",exists);
//wrap the true or false return into the JsValue structure and
return it
JsValue::from_serde(&exists).unwrap()
}
```

Before compiling, you need to modify the Cargo.toml file to input the dependencies.

The following shows a Cargo.toml file. Change the crate-type if needed and the dependencies section.

```
[package]
name = "cuckoo"
version = "0.1.0"
edition = "2018"
[lib]
crate-type = ["cdylib"]
[dependencies]
serde = { version = "1.0", features = ["derive"] }
wasm-bindgen = { version = "0.2", features = ["serde-
serialize"] }
cuckoofilter = "0.3"
lazy_static = "1.3.0"
```

The file includes dependencies for a cuckoo filter, crate, wasm-bindgen, serde (serialization and deserialization), and lazy static. Under lib, you need to make the crate-type cdylib, which is done to compile to a library like a DLL file for a normal compilation target, but in this case, you generate a Wasm file.

cargo.toml file

Once this is done, compile the code with wasm32 as the target.

cargo build --target wasm32-unknown-unknown

You see a screen like the one shown in Figure 4-3.

```
root@INLN34327424A:/home/ubuntu/cuckoo# cargo build --target wasm32-unknown-unknown
    Updating crates.io index
  Downloaded serde_json v1.0.66
  Downloaded 1 crate (115.1 KB) in 12.17s
   Compiling proc-macro2 v1.0.28
   Compiling unicode-xid v0.2.2
   Compiling syn v1.0.74
   Compiling log v0.4.14
   Compiling wasm-bindgen-shared v0.2.74
   Compiling serde_derive v1.0.126
   Compiling cfg-if v1.0.0
   Compiling ryu v1.0.5
   Compiling libc v0.2.98
   Compiling serde v1.0.126
   Compiling lazy_static v1.4.0
   Compiling bumpalo v3.7.0
   Compiling serde_json v1.0.66
   Compiling rand v0.4.6
   Compiling itoa v0.4.7
   Compiling wasm-bindgen v0.2.74
   Compiling byteorder v0.5.3
   Compiling quote v1.0.9
   Compiling rand v0.3.23
   Compiling cuckoofilter v0.3.2
   Compiling wasm-bindgen-backend v0.2.74
   Compiling wasm-bindgen-macro-support v0.2.74
   Compiling wasm-bindgen-macro v0.2.74
    Building [========================>    ] 41/46: serde_derive
```

Figure 4-3. *Building Rust code in progress*

The cuckoo.wasm file is under target/wasm32-unknown-unknown/
debug/ in the directory tree (see Figure 4-4).

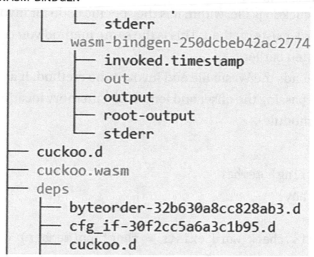

Figure 4-4. *Directory tree showing the compiled Wasm file*

Now it's time to generate the JavaScript stubs and modified Wasm
using the wasm-bindgen utility.

Let's use the wasm-bindgen to generate the needed stubs and target as
Node.js. Target as Node.js means the generated JavaScript file can be run
within the Node.js engine.

Run the following command from within the root directory of the
cuckoo project.

```
wasm-bindgen target/wasm32-unknown-unknown/debug/cuckoo.
wasm  --target nodejs --out-dir .
```

Listing the generated files, you see the following files.

```
Cargo.lock  Cargo.toml  cuckoo.d.ts  cuckoo.js  cuckoo_
bg.wasm  cuckoo_bg.wasm.d.ts  src  target
```

The generated files are shown in bold and italics, including the
modified Wasm file and the stubs for the glue code for Node.js to invoke
Wasm with the string type.

Open the cuckoo.js file; within it is the specific code for invocation of the check_word_exists method. This is the same method you created in the Rust code written earlier.

The code loads the Wasm file and invokes the method. It also explains the method is passing the offset and length of a memory location to the guest (Wasm module).

```
/**
 * @param {string} member
 * @returns {any}
 */
module.exports.check_word_exists = function(member) {
    var ptr0 = passStringToWasm0(member, wasm.__wbindgen_
    malloc, wasm.__wbindgen_realloc);
    var len0 = WASM_VECTOR_LEN;
    var ret = wasm.check_word_exists(ptr0, len0);
    return takeObject(ret);
};
```

The cuckoo filter checks the presence of the keyword in the cuckoo filter. The filter is preloaded with a few keys, which is defined in the Rust code.

```
let words = vec!["foo", "bar", "xylophone", "milagro"];
```

Create an app.js file that imports the cuckoo.js file.

```
const {check_word_exists}=require('./cuckoo.js')
console.log(check_word_exists("foo"));
```

Run the app.js file with the following command.

```
node app.js
```

You should get true as the value.

Next, change app.js to pass a key that does not exist in the cuckoo filter, as follows.

```
console.log(check_word_exists("test"));
```

You get false as the answer from the Wasm module.

Summary

This chapter began with the wasm-bindgen tool, which allows JavaScript programs to interface with WebAssembly. Since you know WebAssembly only allows numeric types to be exchanged between host and guest, you need a mechanism that allows you to encode and decode the complex types into numeric types. This heavy lifting is done by the wasm-bindgen tool for only JavaScript-based hosts like Node.js.

The chapter also covered cuckoo filters and probabilistic data structures and showed you how to code a simple cuckoo filter in Rust and expose the same as a Wasm module. In addition, you learned how to generate stubs for the same module using wasm-bindgen and then consume the same via a Node.js program.

CHAPTER 5

waPC

In Chapter 4, you saw how wasm-bindgen generates stubs to communicate between JavaScript and Rust-based Wasm and vice versa. However, since wasm-bindgen only allows JavaScript as a host, you must look at approaches that allow interoperability between a Rust-based host and a Golang-based host.

This chapter looks at alternative means of achieving communication between different host runtimes and Wasm modules. The host runtime used here is based on Rust, Golang, and Node.js. The approach explains generating Wasm via the waPC toolchain and then using waPC bindings for different host runtimes.

waPC Architecture

waPC (WebAssembly Procedure Calls) achieves communication between the host and the guest, as shown in Figure 5-1.

© Shashank Mohan Jain 2022

S. M. Jain, *WebAssembly for Cloud*, https://doi.org/10.1007/978-1-4842-7496-5_5

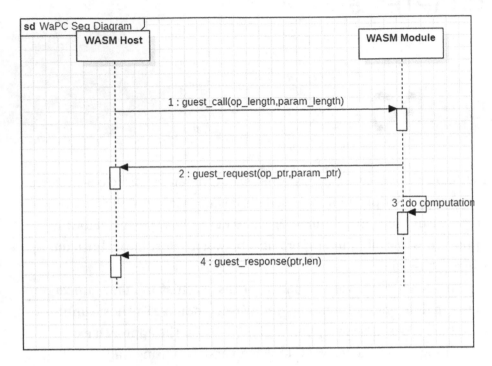

Figure 5-1. *waPC architecture*

Let's look at Figure 5-1 step by step.

1. The host invokes a function call guest_call on the Wasm module. It passes the length of operation and length of the parameter as input.

2. On receiving this call, the guest invokes a guest_ request method on the host runtime. It passes the pointer to the operation in the guest memory and the pointer to the parameter. Since the host has access to the guest memory, it can populate the data in that location.

3. Once the guest_request method succeeds, which means that the host has set the right data into the specified memory locations, the guest can perform the operation with the parameter passed.

4. The guest invokes guest response method on host passing the pointer (offset) and length of response it populated in memory for the host to discover and decode the response.

This example is another way to pass complex types like strings as a parameter to the functions exposed by the Wasm module.

Since you now understand that this mechanism like wasm-bindgen would need changes to both host (in terms of the glue code) and the Wasm file for facilitating encoding and decoding of the parameters for operations on guest module from the host or vice versa.

Next, you learn how to use waPC to generate these stubs in Node.js, Rust, and Golang. I explain how to create the Wasm module using waPC and show you the source code for invoking the guest module via Node.js. The prerequisites are to have Node and npm installed.

```
Install wapc cli
wget -q https://raw.githubusercontent.com/wapc/cli/master/
install/install.sh -O - | /bin/bash
```

Once they are installed, you see in following output. (The system here is linux_amd64.)

```
waPC CLI is detected:
wapc version 0.0.4 linux/amd64
Reinstalling waPC CLI - /usr/local/bin/wapc...

Getting the latest waPC CLI...
Installing v0.0.4 waPC CLI...
```

```
Downloading https://github.com/wapc/cli/releases/download/
v0.0.4/wapc_linux_amd64.tar.gz ...
[sudo] password for ubuntu:
wapc installed into /usr/local/bin successfully.
wapc version 0.0.4 linux/amd64
```

waPC CLI is installed successfully.

Now let's discuss how to take the same Rust project you used with wasm-bindgen and turn it into a waPC-compliant project.

```
Check installation version
ubuntu@INLN34327424A:~$ wapc version
wapc version 0.0.4 linux/amd64
```

Create a waPC-based Rust project.

```
ubuntu@INLN34327424A:~$ wapc new rust cuckoo_wapc
```

```
Creating project directory /home/ubuntu/cuckoo_wapc
```

Please enter the project description: cuckoo filter in Rust using waPC.
Please enter the version (the default is 0.0.1).
The cuckoo_wapc directory is created and under it are the following files.

```
Cargo.toml  Makefile  codegen.yaml  schema.widl  src
```

First is the schema.widl file. This file defines the interface of the function you expose from the Wasm module. Open the default schema. widl file. You see the following content.

```
namespace "greeting"

interface {
  sayHello(name: string): string
}
```

This means you expose a sayHello method from the Wasm module. This method takes a parameter name with the type as a string and returns a string. Since the example you are supposed to work on is on the cuckoo filter, let's use the method in the wasm-bindgen-based cuckoo filter example. The check_word_exists method takes input as string JSON and output as a string (true or false wrapped in a string).

You modify the schema.widl file as follows.

```
namespace "cuckoo"
interface {
  check_word_exists(name: string): string
}
```

Next, under the src directory, create a lib.rs file and copy the following code. The code is similar to what you saw in the wasm-bindgen example (except for the two methods).

```
// This method is used to register the method check_word_exists
with the Handler
#[no_mangle]
pub fn wapc_init() {
    Handlers::register_check_word_exists(check_word_exists);
}
// This method now doesn't have the wasm bindgen annotation as
// it had in case of wasm bindgen example. Functionality wise it
// remains same.
fn check_word_exists(member: String) -> HandlerResult<String> {
    let exists = cf.contains(&member);
    println!("{}", exists);
    Ok(exists.to_string())
}
```

The following is the complete code.

```
#[macro_use]
extern crate lazy_static;
mod generated;
extern crate cuckoofilter;
//extern crate wasm_bindgen;
use cuckoofilter::CuckooFilter;
use serde::{Deserialize, Serialize};
use std::collections::hash_map::DefaultHasher;
use std::collections::HashMap;
extern crate wapc_guest as guest;
pub use generated::*;
use guest::prelude::*;

lazy_static! {
    static ref cf: CuckooFilter<DefaultHasher> = {
        let CF: CuckooFilter<DefaultHasher> = load_data();
        CF
    };
}

fn load_data() -> CuckooFilter<DefaultHasher> {
    let words = vec!["foo", "bar", "xylophone", "milagro"];
    let mut CF2: CuckooFilter<DefaultHasher> =
CuckooFilter::new();

    let mut insertions = 0;
    for s in &words {
        if CF2.test_and_add(s) {
            insertions += 1;
        }
```

```
    }
    CF2
}

#[no_mangle]
pub fn wapc_init() {
    Handlers::register_check_word_exists(check_word_exists);
}

fn check_word_exists(member: String) -> HandlerResult<String> {
    let exists = cf.contains(&member);
    println!("{}", exists);
    Ok(exists.to_string())
}

fn say_hello(_name: String) -> HandlerResult<String> {
    Ok("".to_string()) // TODO: Provide implementation.
}
```

Now we check the generated Cargo.toml file

```
[package]
name = "cuckoo_wapc"
version = "0.0.1"
description = "cuckoo filter in rust using wapc"
authors = [""]
edition = "2018"
license = "Apache-2.0"

[lib]
crate-type = ["cdylib", "rlib"]

[features]
default = ["guest"]
guest = []
```

```
[dependencies]
wapc-guest = "0.4.0"
serde = { version = "1.0.115" , features = ["derive"] }
serde_json = "1.0.57"
serde_derive = "1.0.115"
serde_bytes = "0.11.5"
rmp-serde = "0.14.4"
lazy_static = "1.4.0"

[dev-dependencies]
structopt = "0.3.17"
serde_json = "1.0.57"
base64 = "0.12.3"

[profile.release]
# Optimize for small code size
opt-level = "s"
lto = true
```

You need to add some more dependencies under the dependencies section.

```
cuckoofilter = "0.3"
```

The dependencies section now looks like the following.

```
[dependencies]
cuckoofilter = "0.3"
wapc-guest = "0.4.0"
serde = { version = "1.0.115" , features = ["derive"] }
serde_json = "1.0.57"
serde_derive = "1.0.115"
serde_bytes = "0.11.5"
rmp-serde = "0.14.4"
lazy_static = "1.4.0"
```

The make file is also in the project's root directory. Its content is as follows.

```
all: deps codegen build

deps:

codegen:
        wapc generate codegen.yaml

build:
        cargo build --target wasm32-unknown-unknown --release
        mkdir -p build && cp target/wasm32-unknown-unknown/
        release/*.wasm build/

# Rust builds accrue disk space over time (specifically the target
# directory), so running `make clean` should be done periodically.
clean:
        cargo clean
        rm -Rf build

doc:

test: build
        cargo test
```

Essentially, the make file generates the codegen.yaml file and builds the code.

Next, run the make file by running the make command from the root directory of the project. You see a screen similar to the one shown in Figure 5-2 once the build starts.

```
wapc generate codegen.yaml
Generating src/generated.rs...
Skipping src/lib.rs...
Formatting src/generated.rs...
Formatting src/lib.rs...
cargo build --target wasm32-unknown-unknown --release
    Updating crates.io index
  Compiling proc-macro2 v1.0.28
  Compiling unicode-xid v0.2.2
  Compiling syn v1.0.74
  Compiling serde_derive v1.0.126
  Compiling autocfg v1.0.1
  Compiling serde v1.0.126
  Compiling ryu v1.0.5
  Compiling serde_json v1.0.66
  Compiling byteorder v1.4.3
  Compiling lazy_static v1.4.0
  Compiling itoa v0.4.7
  Compiling num-traits v0.2.14
  Compiling wapc-guest v0.4.0
    Building [============>          ] 16/32: wapc-guest, proc-macro2, serde(build), num-traits(build.rs)
```

Figure 5-2. *Build in progress for the Wasm module*

After a successful build, the Wasm file is generated under the directory.

target/wasm32-unknown-unknown/release
The name of the file is cuckoo_wapc.wasm

Now let's create a node JavaScript-based JavaScript file and consume this Wasm module from there.

Before you can invoke the Wasm module from Node.js, you need to install the following dependencies.

Run the following command from the project's root so that the JavaScript file can find the node dependencies.

Install msgpack dependency and wapc dependency
npm install @wapc/host @msgpack/msgpack

Create a file named wapc.js with the following content.

//imports for wapc and messagepack. Wapc uses messagepack as
the binary protocol for encoding.

const { instantiate } = require("@wapc/host");
const { encode, decode } = require("@msgpack/msgpack");

```javascript
const { promises: fs } = require("fs");
const path = require("path");

// Argument as index 0 is the node executable, index 1 is the
   wasm filename

const wasmfile = process.argv[2]; //wasm file as input
const operation = process.argv[3]; // function defined in wasm
                                   file (check_word_exists)
const json = process.argv[4]; //json for input parameters to
                              the function

// If we don't have the basic arguments we need, print usage and exit.
if (!(wasmfile && operation && json)) {
  console.log("Usage: node index.js [wasm file] [waPC
  operation] [JSON input]");
  process.exit(1);
}

async function main() {
  // Read wasm off the local disk as Uint8Array
  buffer = await fs.readFile(path.join(__dirname, wasmfile));

  // Instantiate a WapcHost with the bytes read off disk
  const host = await instantiate(buffer);

  // Parse the input JSON and encode as msgpack
  const payload = encode(JSON.parse(json));

  // Invoke the operation in the wasm guest
  const result = await host.invoke(operation, payload);

  // Decode the results using msgpack
  const decoded = decode(result);
```

```
  // log to the console
  console.log(`Result: ${decoded}`);
}

main().catch((err) => console.error(err));
```

Run this program with the necessary input.

```
node wapc.js target/wasm32-unknown-unknown/release/cuckoo_wapc.
wasm check_word_exists '{"name":"foo"}'
Returns true
```

Next, run same program with a word that doesn't exist in the Bloom filter.

```
node wapc.js target/wasm32-unknown-unknown/release/cuckoo_wapc.
wasm check_word_exists '{"name":"testme"}'
Returns false
```

In the preceding example, you saw how to create a waPC-compliant Rust program that exposes a function named check_word_exists, takes a string as input, and returns a string (true or false).

You defined the function's interface in a schema.widl file, modified the Cargo.toml to include the dependency of your Rust program, and invoked the make program to generate Wasm and the stubs, which can encode and decode JSON with MessagePack.

Next, let's move on to a more complex type of input.

Handling a Complex Type

In the same project, replace the contents of the schema.widl file includes one more type and an interface handle_input, which takes the complex type as input.

```
namespace "cuckoo"

interface {
  check_word_exists(name: string): string
}

type Input {
    x: string,
    y: string,
}

interface {
handle_input(inp:Input):string
}
```

Open the lib.rs file under the src directory and add the following code segment (the struct segment)

```
struct Input {
    x: String,
    y: String,
}
```

Next, add the following code segment in the lib.rs file just to the struct segment.

```
#[no_mangle]
pub fn wapc_init() {
    Handlers::register_check_word_exists(check_word_exists);
    Handlers::register_handle_input(handle_input);
}
```

The init() method already existed. You just need to add the register code for the new method you defined.

```
    Handlers::register_handle_input(handle_input);
```

Apart from that you also need to define the structure input which is used within the handle_input method.

Finally, add the handle_input method to the lib.rs file at the end.

```
fn handle_input(inp: generated::Input) -> HandlerResult<String>
{
    let a = &inp.x;
    Ok(a.to_string())
}
```

This method takes the complex input type as input and returns one of its members as output (in the preceding example, you return a value of x).

Generate the stubs by running make file again.

```
node wapc.js target/wasm32-unknown-unknown/release/cuckoo_wapc.
wasm handle_input '{"inp":{"x":"shashank","y":"test"}}'
```

The output is Shashank.

So far, you have seen how to use the waPC tool to generate Wasm from Rust code with bindings and glue code generated by waPC tooling. From a consumption point of view, you've seen the Node.js-based runtime, which is similar to what you achieved with the wasm-bindgen tooling.

From here, you develop an understanding of generating the bindings for Rust and Golang-based runtimes which can then consume the same Wasm module (cuckoo_wapc.wasm) and invoke the check_word_exists function on it.

Rust Host for waPC-based Bindings

You have used Node.js as the runtime for running the host code and stubs. Node.js comes with an embedded Wasm runtime which loads Wasm and invokes the functions on Wasm. You saw many examples of this in previous sections.

Since you now want to use Rust as the host for invoking the guest, you need to embed a Wasm runtime in the Rust code, which can load the Wasm module and then invoke a function within that Wasm module. waPC comes with support for Wasmtime as the Wasm runtime. You are embedding the Wasmtime engine within the host Rust code. This code does the following.

- Loads the Wasm file into the Wasmtime runtime

- Invokes the check_word_exists function on the Wasm module

The following steps create a Rust-based host with an embedded Wasmtime WebAssembly engine.

1. First, create a Rust project named invoker using the cargo command.

   ```
   cargo new invoker
   ```

2. Replace the content of the src/main.rs file as follows.

   ```
   extern crate wapc;
   extern crate wasmtime_provider;
   extern crate wascc_codec;
   extern crate serde_json;
   extern crate serde_derive;
   extern crate serdeconv;
   use std::collections::HashMap;
   use std::fs::read;
   use std::env;
   use wapc::WapcHost;

   fn runs_wapc_guest() -> anyhow::Result<()> {

     let args: Vec<String> = env::args().collect();
   ```

```
    let wasmpath= &args[1];
    //wasm file path. We will use the cuckoo wasm path here
    let key = &args[2]; //name of the json key
let val= &args[3]; // value

let mut scores = HashMap::new();
// create a hashmap and insert the key value pair
    scores.insert(key.to_string(),val.to_string());

// convert the key value to  message pack
let p2=serdeconv::to_msgpack_vec(&scores).unwrap();
    let buf = read(wasmpath.to_string())?;

// This code creates the wasmtime Engine

    let engine = wasmtime_provider::WasmtimeEngine
    Provider::new(&buf, None);

// We use the wapc wrapper over the wasmtime engine here.
    let guest = WapcHost::new(Box::new(engine), move
|_a, _b, _c, _d, _e| Ok(vec![]))?;

// we invoke the function check_word_exists here and
pass the msgpack encoded message
    let callresult = guest.call("check_word_exists",
    &p2).unwrap();

// response is also encoded by msgpack, so we need to
get the string back from it.
let p1:String=serdeconv::from_msgpack_
slice(&callresult[..]).unwrap();
println!("response{:?}",&p1);
    Ok(())
}
```

```
pub fn main() -> Result<(), Box<dyn std::error::Error>>
{
runs_wapc_guest();

    Ok(())
}
```

3. Replace the content of the Cargo.toml file.

```
[package]
name = "invoker"
version = "0.1.0"
edition = "2018"

# See more keys and their definitions at https://doc.
rust-lang.org/cargo/reference/manifest.html

[dependencies]
wasmtime = "0.24.0"
wapc="0.10.1"
wasmtime-wasi = "0.24.0"
wasmtime-provider="0.0.3"
anyhow = "1.0.31"
wascc-codec = "0.9.1"
serde = "1.0.126"
serde_json = "1.0.41"
serdeconv="0.4.0"
serde_derive = "1.0.126"
[dev-dependencies]
wascc-codec="0.9.1"
env_logger = "0.8.3"
```

4. Build the program using the following command.

```
cargo build
```

```
Compiling crossbeam-epoch v0.9.5
Compiling rayon-core v1.9.1
Compiling once_cell v1.8.0
Compiling scopeguard v1.1.0
Compiling quick-error v1.2.3
Compiling gimli v0.25.0
Compiling ipnet v2.3.1
Compiling regex-syntax v0.6.25
Compiling maybe-owned v0.3.4
Compiling adler v1.0.2
Compiling rustc-demangle v0.1.20
Compiling zstd-safe v3.0.1+zstd.1.4.9
Compiling termcolor v1.1.2
Compiling pin-project-lite v0.2.7
Compiling ryu v1.0.5
Compiling ppv-lite86 v0.2.10
Compiling wasi-common v0.24.0
Compiling wasmtime-cache v0.24.0
Compiling cpufeatures v0.1.5
Compiling serde_json v1.0.66
Compiling opaque-debug v0.3.0
Compiling cpp_demangle v0.3.3
Compiling base64 v0.13.0
Compiling paste v1.0.5
Compiling wasmtime-wasi v0.24.0
Compiling indexmap v1.7.0
Compiling memoffset v0.6.4
Compiling miniz_oxide v0.4.4
Compiling rayon v1.5.1
Compiling num-traits v0.2.14
Compiling pest v2.1.3
Compiling tracing-core v0.1.18
Compiling wast v35.0.2
Compiling wast v36.0.0
Compiling itertools v0.10.1
Compiling heck v0.3.3
Compiling generic-array v0.14.4
Compiling humantime v1.3.0
Compiling addr2line v0.16.0
  Building [=======>                ] 93/244: wast, memoffset(build), miniz_oxide(build), libc
```

Figure 5-3. *Build in progress for the Rust program*

5. Execute it using the following command. (Make sure that the path contains the generated cuckoo_wapc. wasm file.)

```
./target/debug/invoker /home/ubuntu/cuckoo_wapc/
target/wasm32-unknown-unknown/release/cuckoo_
wapc.wasm name foo
Output should be : response"true"
```

```
Try with a wrong input
./target/debug/invoker /home/ubuntu/cuckoo_wapc/
target/wasm32-unknown-unknown/release/cuckoo_
wapc.wasm name xyz
Output should be : response"false"
```

You saw examples of using Node.js as host to the Wasm module, and then you saw Rust embedding the Wasmtime engine and executing the Wasm module. Now, let's move on to a Golang-based runtime.

The prerequisites for this are Go version 1.16.6.

waPC supports Wasmer as the Wasm engine runtime. You need to install the Wasmer runtime on the Ubuntu machine so that the needed libraries like libwasmer can be located by your program.

You can install Wasmer using the following command.

```
curl https://get.wasmer.io -sSfL | sh
```

This installs Wasmer from the following git repository.

```
https://github.com/wasmerio/wasmer
```

Once the initial setup is ready, create a folder called gostandalone on the Ubuntu machine.

In this directory, create a file called main.go.

Copy the content of main.go as follows.

```
package main

import (
        "context"
        "fmt"
        "io/ioutil"
        "os"
        "github.com/wapc/wapc-go"
        json2msgpack "github.com/izinin/json2msgpack"
)
```

```go
//var  instance  wasm.Instance
var ctx context.Context
func main() {
        if len(os.Args) < 2 {
                fmt.Println("usage: hello <name>")
                return
        }
        wasm:=os.Args[1]
        funcname := os.Args[2]
        name:=os.Args[3]
        ctx := context.Background()
        code, err := ioutil.ReadFile(wasm)
        if err != nil {
                panic(err)
        }

        module, err := wapc.New(code,nil)
        if err != nil {
                panic(err)
        }

        defer module.Close()

        instance, err := module.Instantiate()
        if err != nil {
                panic(err)
        }
        defer instance.Close()
        b:=json2msgpack.EncodeJSON([]byte(name))

        result, err := instance.Invoke(ctx, funcname, b)
        if err != nil {
                panic(err)
```

```
        }

        fmt.Println(string(result))
}
```

Execute the following commands.

```
go mod init main.go
go mod tidy
```

These two generate two files: go.mod and go.sum.

Finally, you build the Go binary using the following command.

```
go build -o cuckoo
```

This generates a binary named cuckoo.

You can now execute the binary passing the needed arguments.

```
./cuckoo /home/ubuntu/cuckoo_wapc/target/wasm32-unknown-
unknown/release/cuckoo_wapc.wasm check_word_exists
'{"name":"foo"}'
```

Here first argument is the cuckoo_wapc.wasm you generated earlier in the chapter.

Second argument is the function to be invoked on Wasm (check_word_exists).

And final argument is the JSON to be passed ('{"name":"foo"}').

The output results in true as foo exists within the cuckoo filter.

You then run a negative scenario by passing something which doesn't exist in cuckoo filter.

```
./cuckoo /home/ubuntu/cuckoo_wapc/target/wasm32-unknown-
unknown/release/cuckoo_wapc.wasm check_word_exists
'{"name":"xyz"}'
```

This results in false as the output.

Summary

This chapter discussed WebAssembly Procedure Calls (waPC). First, you learned how to use waPC to create a Wasm module that can pass complex types between a Wasm host and guest. From there, you learned how to invoke the Wasm module from three different runtimes: Node.js, Rust, and Golang.

After this chapter, you should be able to use waPC to create your own Wasm modules to handle complex types and execute them in any of these runtimes.

CHAPTER 6

Wasm Web Interface

In previous chapters, you learned how to use the stand-alone mode of your programs to launch the Wasm module and invoke functions on it from the host.

This chapter takes you through the journey of taking a Wasm module and exposing it over an HTTP-based interface, which means that the Wasm module is launched on the arrival of an HTTP request. Wasm is a great candidate for cloud computing because each Wasm module is a small sandbox of code. You can run multitenant code on the same Linux process and achieve a good amount of isolation using the Wasm mechanism.

As many workloads also adopt a serverless way of packaging and running them, the Wasm paradigm finds a sweet spot in the serverless world. You can easily package the workloads as Wasm modules that can then be loaded by your Wasm runtime of choice on the cloud and the exposed functions invoked on them. This achieves true on-demand computing, as is the aspiration of any cloud platform.

As was the approach in previous chapters, let's start by taking the cuckoo filter Wasm module and serve it over an HTTP server in Rust.

The following are the goals of this program.

1. Load the Wasm engine at the start of the server so that you don't load it on individual requests.

2. Listen at an HTTP endpoint to serve HTTP-based requests.

© Shashank Mohan Jain 2022
S. M. Jain, *WebAssembly for Cloud*, https://doi.org/10.1007/978-1-4842-7496-5_6

3. Load the Wasm module into the engine on receipt of
    the HTTP request and invoke the function.

Execute the command shown in Listing 6-1 to create a Rust project
named cuckoo_http.

```
cargo new cuckoo_http
```

Open the main.rs file under the src directory of the cuckoo_http
project.

Listing 6-1. main.rs

```rust
extern crate wasmtime_provider;
pub mod httprequest;
use std::io::prelude::*;
use httprequest::HttpRequest;
use std::net::TcpListener;
use std::net::TcpStream;
use std::env;
extern crate wapc;
use wasmtime_provider::WasmtimeEngineProvider;
pub mod wasm;
fn main() {
// create a TCP listener to listen on localhost at port 8080
    let listener = TcpListener::bind("127.0.0.1:8080").
    unwrap();

  let args: Vec<String> = env::args().collect();
// pass the wasm file path as an argument to the program binary
    let wasmpath= &args[1];
// launch the wasm engine with loading the wasm module at start.
```

```
let guest =    wasm::engine_start(wasmpath.to_string()).
unwrap();
// start listening for TCP connections here
    for stream in listener.incoming() {
        let stream = stream.unwrap();
// Handle the TCP request by invoking this method
        handle_connection(stream,&guest);
    }
}
// connection Handler for the TCP connection
fn handle_connection(mut stream: TcpStream,guest:&wapc::
WapcHost) {
    let mut buffer = [0; 512];

    stream.read(&mut buffer).unwrap();
//create an http request from the tcp request.
let req: HttpRequest = String::from_utf8(buffer.to_vec()).
unwrap().into();

let body= &req.msg_body;

println!("body={}",body);

// invoke the method on wasm.rs file and pass the http request
body (key value pair) to it.
let p1=wasm::runs_wapc_guest(&guest,body).unwrap();
let response = format!("HTTP/1.1 200 OK\r\n\r\n{}", p1);
// write the response back
    stream.write(response.as_bytes()).unwrap();
    stream.flush().unwrap();
}
```

Listing 6-2 represents a helper class to extract HTTP headers, body and formulate an HTTP request object from the TCP stream. Place the httprequest.rs file under the src directory of the project.

Listing 6-2. httprequest.rs

```
use std::collections::HashMap;
#[derive(Debug, PartialEq)]
pub enum Resource {
    Path(String),
}
// HttpRequest Object definition
#[derive(Debug)]
pub struct HttpRequest {
    pub method: Method,
    pub version: Version,
    pub resource: Resource,
    pub headers: HashMap<String, String>,
    pub msg_body: String,
}

impl From<String> for HttpRequest {
    fn from(req: String) -> Self {
        let mut parsed_method = Method::Uninitialized;
        let mut parsed_version = Version::V1_1;
        let mut parsed_resource = Resource::Path
        ("".to_string());
        let mut parsed_headers = HashMap::new();
        let mut parsed_msg_body = "";

        // Read each line in incoming HTTP request
        for line in req.lines() {
```

```
    // If the line read is request line, call function
       process_req_line()
    if line.contains("HTTP") {
        let (method, resource, version) = process_req_
        line(line);
        parsed_method = method;
        parsed_version = version;
        parsed_resource = resource;
    // If the line read is header line, call function
       process_header_line()
    } else if line.contains(":") {
        let (key, value) = process_header_line(line);
        parsed_headers.insert(key, value);
    //  If it is blank line, do nothing
    } else if line.len() == 0 {
        // If none of these, treat it as message body
    } else {
        parsed_msg_body = line;
    }
}
// Parse the incoming HTTP request into HttpRequest
   struct
HttpRequest {
    method: parsed_method,
    version: parsed_version,
    resource: parsed_resource,
    headers: parsed_headers,
    msg_body: parsed_msg_body.to_string(),
}

}

}
```

```
//fn process_req_line(s: &str) -> (Method, Resource, Version) {}
fn process_req_line(s: &str) -> (Method, Resource, Version) {
    // Parse the request line into individual chunks split by
       whitespaces.
    let mut words = s.split_whitespace();
    // Extract the HTTP method from first part of the request line
    let method = words.next().unwrap();
    // Extract the resource (URI/URL) from second part of the
       request line
    let resource = words.next().unwrap();
    // Extract the HTTP version from third part of the request line
    let version = words.next().unwrap();

    (
        method.into(),
        Resource::Path(resource.to_string()),
        version.into(),
    )
}

// method for processing http headers
fn process_header_line(s: &str) -> (String, String) {
    // Parse the headerline into words split by separator (':')
    let mut header_items = s.split(":");
    let mut key = String::from("");
    let mut value = String::from("");
    // Extract the key part of the header
    if let Some(k) = header_items.next() {
        key = k.to_string();
    }
```

```rust
    // Extract the value part of the header
    if let Some(v) = header_items.next() {
        value = v.to_string()
    }

    (key, value)
}

#[derive(Debug, PartialEq)]
pub enum Method {
    Get,
    Post,
    Uninitialized,
}
impl From<&str> for Method {
    fn from(s: &str) -> Method {
        match s {
            "GET" => Method::Get,
            "POST" => Method::Post,
            _ => Method::Uninitialized,
        }
    }
}
#[derive(Debug, PartialEq)]
pub enum Version {
    V1_1,
    V2_0,
    Uninitialized,
}
impl From<&str> for Version {
    fn from(s: &str) -> Version {
        match s {
            "HTTP/1.1" => Version::V1_1,
```

```
        _ => Version::Uninitialized,
    }
  }
}
```

Finally, create the wasm.rs file within the src directory, which is responsible for starting the Wasm engine and then invoking the guest module. Listing 6-3 shows this.

Listing 6-3. wasm.rs

```
extern crate wapc;
extern crate wasmtime_provider;
extern crate wascc_codec;
extern crate serde_json;
extern crate serde_derive;
extern crate serdeconv;
use std::collections::HashMap;
use std::fs::read;
use std::env;
use wapc::WapcHost;
use std::error::Error;
use wasmtime_provider::WasmtimeEngineProvider;
//use std::collections::HashMap;
// this method accepts the path of the wasm file as input. This
// starts the engine and loads the wasm module.
pub fn engine_start(wasmpath:String) -> Result<WapcHost,
Box<dyn Error>>
{
  let args: Vec<String> = env::args().collect();

    let buf = read(wasmpath.to_string())?;

    let engine = wasmtime_provider::WasmtimeEngineProvider::new
    (&buf, None);
```

```
    let guest = WapcHost::new(Box::new(engine), move |_a, _b,
    _c, _d, _e| Ok(vec![]))?;
Ok(guest)

}

// this method gets the request body (key value pair). It
// creates a hashmap entry for the key value encodes it via
// msgpack and then passes the encoded message to the wasm module

pub fn runs_wapc_guest(guest:&WapcHost,body:&String) ->
Result<String, Box<dyn Error>> {
//let guest = WapcHost::new(Box::new(*engine), move |_a, _b,
_c, _d, _e| Ok(vec![]))?;
let res: Vec<String> = body.split("=").map(|s| s.to_string()).
collect();
//let mut scores = one_liner(body);
let mut scores = HashMap::new();
let x=&res[0];
let y=&res[1];
scores.insert(x.trim_matches(char::from(0)).to_string(),y.trim_
matches(char::from(0)).to_string());

println!("key={}",&res[0]);
println!("value={}",&res[1]);
println!("map{:?}",&scores);
//msgpack encoding is done here
let p2=serdeconv::to_msgpack_vec(&scores).unwrap();
// invoke the check_word_exists method on wasm module and pass
the encoded message
let callresult = &guest.call("check_word_exists", &p2).
unwrap();
```

```
// decode the msgpack encoded response back to string
let p1:String=serdeconv::from_msgpack_slice(&callresult[..]).unwrap();
println!("response{:?}",&p1);
    Ok(p1)
}
```

Copy the content from the following file for the Cargo.toml file.

```
[package]
name = "cuckoo_http"
version = "0.1.0"
edition = "2018"

# See more keys and their definitions at https://doc.rust-lang.
org/cargo/reference/manifest.html

[dependencies]
wasmtime = "0.24.0"
wapc="0.10.1"
wasmtime-wasi = "0.24.0"
wasmtime-provider="0.0.3"
anyhow = "1.0.31"
wascc-codec = "0.9.1"
serde = "1.0.126"
serde_json = "1.0.41"
serdeconv="0.4.0"
serde_derive = "1.0.126"
lazy_static = "0.1.*"
futures = { version = "0.3.6", default-features = false,
features = ["async-await"] }
hyper = "0.13"
tokio = { version = "0.2", features = ["macros", "rt-threaded"] }
```

```
route-recognizer = "0.2"
bytes = "0.5"
async-trait = "0.1"
[dev-dependencies]
wascc-codec="0.9.1"
env_logger = "0.8.3"
```

Once these files are created, build the code using the following command.

```
cargo build
```

```
Compiling cc v1.0.69
Compiling rand_core v0.6.3
Compiling mio v0.6.23
Compiling rmp v0.8.10
Compiling regex v1.5.4
Compiling rustc_version v0.3.3
Compiling io-lifetimes v0.1.1
Compiling system-interface v0.6.6
Compiling digest v0.9.0
Compiling block-buffer v0.9.0
Compiling shellexpand v2.1.0
Compiling rand_chacha v0.3.1
Compiling zstd-sys v1.4.20+zstd.1.4.9
Compiling psm v0.1.14
Compiling backtrace v0.3.61
Compiling wasmtime-runtime v0.24.0
Compiling wasmtime-fiber v0.24.0
Compiling crossbeam-deque v0.8.0
Compiling env_logger v0.7.1
Compiling unsafe-io v0.6.12
Compiling cap-primitives v0.13.10
Compiling cap-std v0.13.10
Compiling cap-fs-ext v0.13.10
Compiling sha2 v0.9.5
Compiling rand v0.8.4
Compiling thiserror-impl v1.0.26
Compiling tracing-attributes v0.1.15
Compiling scroll_derive v0.10.5
Compiling pin-project-internal v1.0.8
Compiling tokio-macros v0.2.6
Compiling trackable_derive v1.0.0
Compiling file-per-thread-logger v0.1.4
Compiling cap-rand v0.13.10
Compiling thiserror v1.0.26
Compiling tracing v0.1.26
Compiling scroll v0.10.2
Compiling tokio v0.2.25
Compiling pin-project v1.0.8
Compiling trackable v1.2.0
Compiling witx v0.9.1
Compiling futures v0.3.16
Compiling tracing-futures v0.2.5
 Building [==================>         ] 238/301: rayon, indexmap, zstd-sys(build), wasmtime-fiber(build), witx, tokio
```

Figure 6-1. *Building the Rust program*

If there are no errors, you can see the executable under

`target/debug` directory and the executable name would be `cuckoo_http`

You can launch the HTTP server by passing the Wasm file path as follows. The cuckoo.wasm file is the same as the one you created in Chapter 5.

```
./target/debug/cuckoo_http ../cuckoo_wapc/target/wasm32-
unknown-unknown/release/cuckoo_wapc.wasm
```

Now open another shell to make an HTTP request to this HTTP server via cURL.

```
curl -d "name=foo" -X GET "http://localhost:8080"
```

Figure 6-2 shows two parts.

- On the right, a cURL call is made to the HTTP endpoint.

- On the left, the Rust HTTP server handles the request by invoking Wasm.

Figure 6-2. *Rust HTTP server app and cURL-based HTTP client*

So far, you have seen how to embed a Wasm engine in Rust and run it within an HTTP server. You also saw how to consume the Wasm module over an HTTP-based endpoint. You now take the same Wasm module and expose it via a node-based HTTP endpoint.

Node Example

The previous section exposed a cuckoo filter–based Wasm module over an HTTP interface. You now use a Node.js-based runtime and expose the same Wasm module over an HTTP interface based on node.

Create a directory called node_cuckoo_http.

Under that directory, create a cuckoo.js file and copy and paste the following code into it.

```
// import the needed dependencies for wapc and msgpack

const { instantiate } = require("@wapc/host");
const { encode, decode } = require("@msgpack/msgpack");
const { promises: fs } = require("fs");
const http = require('http');
const path = require("path");
const url = require("url");
// Argument as index 0 is the node executable
// index 1 is the path to wasm file name
const wasmfile = process.argv[2];
// index 2 is the name of operation (in our case check_word_exists)
const operation = process.argv[3];
var host=null;
var buffer=null;
// If we don't have the basic arguments we need, print usage and exit.
```

```
if (!(wasmfile && operation )) {
  console.log("Usage: node index.js [wasm file] [waPC
  operation]");
  process.exit(1);
}

// start of main function
async function main() {
console.log("entered main");
  // Read wasm off the local disk as Uint8Array
buffer = await fs.readFile(path.join(__dirname, wasmfile));

  // Instantiate a WapcHost with the bytes read off disk
   host = await instantiate(buffer);
console.log("host initiated");
const server = http.createServer(requestListener);
console.log("server created and listening for tcp connections
on port 8080");
server.listen(8080);
}
// http request listener
 const requestListener = async function (req, res) {

// extract the query parameter from the http request
let query = url.parse(req.url, true).query;
    console.log(query.key);
// get the value of the parameter key (value for this key is the json)
const payload = encode(JSON.parse(query.key));

  // Invoke the operation in the wasm guest
  const result = await   host.invoke(operation, payload);
  // Decode the results using msgpack
```

```
const decoded = decode(result);

// log to the console
console.log(`Result: ${decoded}`);
res.writeHead(200);
res.end('result='+decoded);
}
```

```
main().catch((err) => console.error(err));with http
```

Before starting the program, make sure you have the following node modules installed in the same directory as the cuckoo.js file. Use the following commands to install the following dependencies.

```
npm install @wapc/host @msgpack/msgpack
```

Start the program.

```
node cuckoo.js ../cuckoo_wapc/target/wasm32-unknown-unknown/
release/cuckoo_wapc.wasm check_word_exists
```

The preceding command starts an HTTP server which loads the Wasm module (cuckoo_wapc.wasm) into the Wasm runtime provided by Node.js. You also pass the function to be invoked as a command-line argument to the server.

Once the HTTP server is up and running, it's time to make an HTTP request via cURL from a second shell. Here, you pass the JSON as a query parameter that the Node.js server handles. It does the following.

1. Extracts the JSON

2. Encodes it into MessagePack

3. Invokes the check_word_exists function on the Wasm module

4. Returns true or false as a result

```
curl  -G -i "http://localhost:8080" --data-urlencode
'key={"name":"foo"}'
```

The output would be similar to the following.

```
ubuntu@INLN34327424A:~$ curl  -G -i http://localhost:8080
--data-urlencode 'key={"name":"foo"}'
HTTP/1.1 200 OK
Date: Tue, 31 Aug 2021 10:28:41 GMT
Connection: keep-alive
Keep-Alive: timeout=5
Transfer-Encoding: chunked
```

result=trueubuntu@INLN34327424A:~$

In the previous section, you learned how to create a simple Node.js-based HTTP server and serve the waPC-compliant Wasm module over an HTTP request. This section demonstrates how to create an HTTP server in Golang and serve the same Wasm module over an HTTP interface.

```
Prerequisites : go 1.16
```
Approach

Create a go_cuckoo_http directory and under it, create a main.go file. Copy the content from Listing 6-4.

Listing 6-4. main.go

```
package main

import (
        "context"

        "io/ioutil"
        "os"
        "log"
        "net/http"
```

```go
        "github.com/wapc/wapc-go"

        json2msgpack "github.com/izinin/json2msgpack"
)
var ctx context.Context
func main() {
        wasmname := os.Args[1]
        functionname := os.Args[2]
        code, err := ioutil.ReadFile(wasmname)
        if err != nil {
                panic(err)
        }

        module, err := wapc.New(code,nil)
        if err != nil {
                panic(err)
        }

        defer module.Close()

        instance, err := module.Instantiate()
        if err != nil {
                panic(err)
        }
        defer instance.Close()

        http.HandleFunc("/", testHandler(instance,functionname))
        log.Fatal(http.ListenAndServe(":8080", nil))
}

func testHandler(instance *wapc.Instance, functionname string )
http.HandlerFunc {
return func (w http.ResponseWriter, r *http.Request) {
```

```
    keys, ok := r.URL.Query()["key"]
  ctx := context.Background()
    if !ok || len(keys[0]) < 1 {
        log.Println("Url Param 'key' is missing")
        return
    }

    // Query()["key"] will return an array of items,
    // we only want the single item.
    key := keys[0]

b:=json2msgpack.EncodeJSON([]byte(key))

//          fmt.Println(b)

        result, err := instance.Invoke(ctx, functionname, b)
        if err != nil {
                panic(err)
        }
w.Write([]byte(result))
//          fmt.Println(w, string(result))
}
}
```

Once the content is copied run the following commands
Run the below set of command
go mod init main.go
go mod tidy

This generates two files: go.mod and go.sum.
The go.mod file has the following content.

```
module main.go
require (
        github.com/izinin/json2msgpack v0.0.0-20171109104254-
        58b3991b6103
```

```
        github.com/tinylib/msgp v1.1.6 // indirect
        github.com/wapc/wapc-go v0.3.0
)
```

Once you have these files in place, it's time to build the go project.
Run the following command.

```
go build -o cuckoo_http
```

This should generate a cuckoo_http binary file under the directory.
You can now start the go-based HTTP server with the following command.

```
./cuckoo_http ../cuckoo_wapc/target/wasm32-unknown-unknown/
release/cuckoo_wapc.wasm check_word_exists
```

The executable is passing two arguments.

- The Wasm file path

- The function exposed from the Wasm file

Once the HTTP server starts, you can test the Wasm module over the
HTTP endpoint from another shell.

```
curl  -G -i "http://localhost:8080" --data-urlencode
'key={"name":"bar"}'
```

This should return true as the response back from the Golang-based
HTTP server.
The output is as follows.

```
ubuntu@INLN34327424A:~$ curl  -G -i http://localhost:8080
--data-urlencode 'key={"name":"bar"}'
HTTP/1.1 200 OK
Date: Tue, 31 Aug 2021 12:07:31 GMT
Content-Length: 5
Content-Type: text/plain; charset=utf-8

true ubuntu@INLN34327424A:~$
```

Summary

In this chapter, you learned how to create an HTTP server in Node.js, Rust, and Golang. You also learned how to embed a Wasm runtime within these HTTP servers. Based on this, you saw how to launch a Wasm module within these HTTP servers. You saw a demonstration on how to invoke these Wasm modules from an HTTP client like cURL. You continued using the same Wasm module you created using the waPC framework and saw how to create Wasm modules and serve them over an HTTP interface in HTTP servers based on Rust, Golang, or Node.js. This opens a different computing paradigm as you can see that the Wasm module itself was written in Rust but is now available to be executed within languages like node and Golang. And not only that, it can now be consumed over an HTTP interface, which makes it a great candidate for microservices and cloud-based development.

## CHAPTER 7

Wasm and Kubernetes

This chapter covers the world of container orchestration via Kubernetes. It explains how to containerize the Wasm-based workloads you developed in Node.js, Rust, and Golang and then deploy them on Kubernetes. You also see how to enable access to them via the Kubernetes service concept.

Before diving into the Wasm side of it, let's discuss Docker and Kubernetes and what they provide for cloud-based workload deployments.

Docker

Docker is among the most promising technologies. It created a revolution in the way workloads are deployed in the cloud. Before the emergence of Docker, virtualization was mainly driven by using virtual machines as the unit for software deployment. Today, Docker is one of the leading technologies for software packaging and deployment on the cloud.

Docker is a Linux-based, open source containerization platform that developers use to build, run, and package applications for deployment using containers. Unlike virtual machines, Docker containers offer the following.

- OS-level abstraction with optimum resource utilization

- Interoperability

© Shashank Mohan Jain 2022
S. M. Jain, *WebAssembly for Cloud*, https://doi.org/10.1007/978-1-4842-7496-5_7

- Efficient build and test

- Faster application execution

Fundamentally, Docker containers modularize an application's functionality into multiple components that allow deploying, testing, or scaling them independently when needed.

Docker provides four fundamental features.

- Images provide a way to package the software optimally. This is achieved by creating layers of software, and common layers are shared between different images. As an example, two Rust-based applications share the majority of Linux user-space libraries and the Rust libraries. This reuse is one of the major attractions of Docker. This saves space not just in the storage of images but also during runtime on the filesystem.

- Containers are the running instances of the images.

- The Docker engine is responsible for running the containers on the host (bare metal or virtual machine). This internally uses many other components like containers, which are beyond the scope of this book. Think of it as an interface for clients to manage the life cycle of the containers.

  A container registry is where all images are stored. There are many container registries in existence today, both public and private.

This book uses Docker Hub as the public registry for our images. You push and pull the images to the registry for storage and retrieval

One of the main selling points of Docker is that it isolates workloads running on the same host. Docker uses three Linux primitives to achieve this: Linux namespaces, csgroups, and layered file systems.

A **namespace** in the Linux kernel sandboxes kernel resources, such as file systems, process trees, message queues, and semaphores and network components like devices, sockets, and routing rules. The idea of namespaces is to isolate processes within their own execution sandbox to run completely isolated from other processes in a different namespace.

There are six major namespaces.

- PID namespace

- Mount namespace

- UTS namespace

- Network namespace

- IPC namespace

- User namespace

Linux namespaces provide isolation from a visibility perspective, and cgroups provide resource accounting (e.g., how much memory or CPU or network a particular process can use).

cgroups is a mechanism in the Linux kernel that provides resource control. This provides a quota of resources like memory, CPU, network I/O to a specific Linux process or a group of processes. Using this mechanism, you can properly manage and assign the resources between the different workloads running on the same host. This helps in proper resource control between multiple tenants running on the same machine.

The **layered file system mechanism** (e.g., aufs or similar) allows you to package the software into different file system layers. This promotes tremendous reuse and a proper packaging mechanism for the software.

So far, you learned that Docker and containers could isolate workloads, provide resource control, and package software. Next, let's look at Kubernetes, a leader in container life cycle managment in terms of deployment and orchestration.

Kubernetes

Docker started a revolution by providing a means to

- Package software

- Provide isolation for tenant software

- Provide resource control for tenants

This revolution needed a way to provide scheduling or, more precisely, an orchestration mechanism to deploy and operate these Docker images. Many such schedulers exist, such as Docker Swarm and HashiCorp Nomad, but the one that had huge acceptance was Kubernetes. Kubernetes came from Google as an open source container orchestration software.

Kubernetes provides a means to deploy software across multiple clouds in a uniform way. This means that the specifics of hyperscale cloud providers like AWS, GCP, and Azure are abstracted out via the Kubernetes API. Software developers don't have to deal with how storage looks on AWS or how networking (software-defined networking) works on GCP. So, you can create Kubernetes-specific deployment files and deploy our software running on top of different cloud environments in a very uniform way.

Kubernetes is designed upfront as a flexible and extensible platform for software deployment. For example, you are not limited to using Docker as the packaging unit for the deployment for the software. There can be alternate technologies like Kata Containers, gVisor, or any other runtime which can be used. Similar extension points exist for networking and storage. Cilium being one example of using an alternate software-defined networking stack on top of Kubernetes.

Kubernetes is mainly based on principles of control theory. Control theory checks the actual state of a system against the desired state of the system. The idea is that the system always moves toward the desired state. This concept is not new. It is evident in biology a process called *homeostasis* and in human inventions like autopilot in cars. To achieve this mechanism, Kubernetes is centered around resources and controllers.

The following are different types of resources.

- Pod: This is the basic unit of deployment in Kubernetes. A pod constitutes one or more Linux containers and shares some namespaces, like network and IPC.

- Deployment: This resource groups a set of pods. For example, you need a minimum of three pods always running for your web application. Create a deployment of size 3. The Kubernetes controllers make sure that you always have three pods running.

```
Take this example
apiVersion: apps/v1
kind: Deployment
metadata:
  name: nginx-deployment
  labels:
    app: nginx
spec:
  replicas: 3
  selector:
    matchLabels:
      app: nginx
  template:
```

```
metadata:
  labels:
    app: nginx
spec:
  containers:
  - name: nginx
    image: nginx:1.14.2
    ports:
    - containerPort: 80
```

There are three pods (called replicas) of nginx configured. So anytime one or more pods goes down, the Kubernetes engine brings it back to the desired state of three pods.

- Service: A service resource abstracts the actual pod IP. Since the pods can be moved to different virtual machines, they don't have a stable IP in the Kubernetes environment. This throws a challenge for the client who wants to connect to that IP (e.g., a pod running a web server on that IP). Kubernetes provides a concept of service to work around this, which provides a stable IP via the magic of mechanisms like Iptables or IPVS. More details on this topic are beyond the scope of this book.

- Stateful set: This resource allows software deployment that requires state-like databases or other storage-backed software. Kubernetes provides a way to deploy these resources so that if the pod moves to a different VM, the same storage is made available on the new machine.

- There are many other resources available, and since Kubernetes is a flexible and extensible environment, it allows one to define custom resources. Controllers in the Kubernetes world manage all these resources. The controller's job is to check the actual state and always move this actual state to the desired state.

The Workings of Kubernetes

A Kubernetes cluster is made of two main components.

- Kubernetes API server for control plane operations

- Nodes that act as hosts for the software deployments like pods

The client interfaces with the Kubernetes API server to manage the life cycle of the different pods deployed across the different virtual machines or nodes. As an example of a deployment of nginx with three replicas, once the request reaches the API server, it becomes the job of the Kubernetes scheduler to see the resources (memory and CPU) availability on different nodes and then place the three pods depending on resource availability.

Each node has an agent running called the *kubelet*, which receives the request to create the containers within the pods. The kubelet is the actual workhorse on the node, which interfaces with runtime API like Docker, Kata Containers, gVisor, or any other container runtime configured.

Further details around Kubernetes are beyond the scope of this book. However, you can find more relevant details at https://kubernetes.io/ or many other Kubernetes resources spread across the web.

This chapter uses two main Kubernetes resources.

- Pod

- Service

The cuckoo filter is deployed as a pod on Kubernetes for two runtimes (Rust, Golang). The node-based runtime is an exercise for you to try on your own.

Next, let's discuss exposing them as a load balancer service in Kubernetes and accessing them from the outside.

Packaging a Rust Web App into a Docker Container

Let's start packaging the Rust-based web app you created in Chapter 6 and package it as a Docker container first.

This section demonstrates how to create a Docker image for a Rust-based web app. This Rust app deploys the Wasm module into the embedded Wasm runtime and makes it available for consumption over an HTTP interface.

Copy the Rust web app project you created in Chapter 6 to a different folder. Create a file named Dockerfile in the same directory. Copy the cuckoo_http.wasm file you generated in that project to the root of this directory.

Copy the content from the following Docker file.

```
FROM rust:1.53.0

# Let's switch our working directory to `app` (equivalent to `cd app`)
# The `app` folder will be created for us by Docker in case it
  does not exist already.
WORKDIR /app
# Copy all files from our working environment to our Docker image
```

```
COPY . .
# Let's build our binary!
# We'll use the release profile to make it fast
RUN cargo build --release
# When `docker run` is executed, launch the binary!
ENTRYPOINT ["./target/release/cuckoo_http", " cuckoo_http.wasm"]
```

The Docker file copies all the files from the directory into the app directory, and a Rust binary is generated. The last line (ENTRYPOINT) starts the binary and passes the Wasm file as the command-line input.

The directory structure should look like in Figure 7-1.

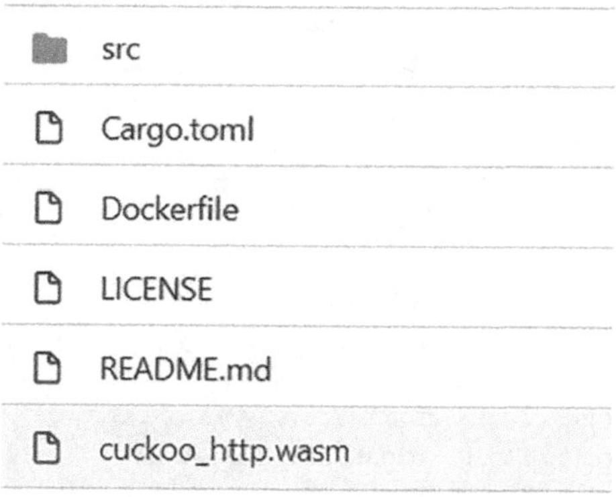

Figure 7-1. *Directory structure for Docker build*

Build the Docker image using the following command.

```
docker build -t <<tagname>> .
```

During the build, you can see all the Rust libraries compiled as the system prepares a binary for the Rust-based web app (see Figure 7-2).

```
Compiling pin-utils v0.1.0
Compiling paste v1.0.5
Compiling pin-project-lite v0.1.12
Compiling futures-channel v0.3.16
Compiling wasmtime-wasi v0.24.0
Compiling httparse v1.4.1
Compiling async-trait v0.1.51
Compiling try-lock v0.2.3
Compiling httpdate v0.3.2
Compiling tower-service v0.3.1
Compiling futures-io v0.3.16
Compiling lazy_static v0.1.16
Compiling route-recognizer v0.2.0
Compiling indexmap v1.7.0
Compiling memoffset v0.6.4
Compiling miniz_oxide v0.4.4
Compiling rayon v1.5.1
Compiling num-traits v0.2.14
Compiling futures-macro v0.3.16
Compiling futures-util v0.3.16
Compiling tracing-core v0.1.18
Compiling pest v2.1.3
Compiling itertools v0.10.1
Compiling wast v35.0.2
Compiling wast v36.0.0
Compiling generic-array v0.14.4
Compiling heck v0.3.3
Compiling humantime v1.3.0
Compiling addr2line v0.16.0
Compiling http v0.2.4
Compiling semver-parser v0.10.2
Compiling quote v1.0.9
Compiling wat v1.0.38
Compiling http-body v0.3.1
Compiling errno v0.2.7
Compiling num_cpus v1.13.0
Compiling atty v0.2.14
Compiling getrandom v0.2.3
Compiling dirs-sys-next v0.1.2
Compiling iovec v0.1.4
Compiling net2 v0.2.37
Compiling socket2 v0.3.19
|
```

Figure 7-2. *Building the Docker image*

After the build, you can check the Dockerized image by the command (see Figure 7-3).

```
docker images
```

```
REPOSITORY              TAG         IMAGE ID         CREATED         SIZE
smjain/rustexample      latest      414f891b1a3b     7 seconds ago   2.3GB
rust                    1.53.0      1ecb70e16851     10 days ago     1.25GB
```

Figure 7-3. *Docker images built in Figure 7-2*

You can validate the Dockerized application by using the Docker run command. (Figure 7-3 shows pushing to the Docker Hub. In my case, it is smjain/rustexample.)

```
docker run -p 8080:8080 <<image id>>
```

A running Docker container can be validated by executing the following command.

```
docker ps
```

Pushing an Image to a Docker Registry

Once you have created the image, you need to push this to a Docker registry. Docker Hub is the registry, and if a user wants to use the Docker Hub, they need to create an account there.

Log in to a Docker registry (Docker Hub) by using the following command.

```
docker login
```

Then, provide the credentials.

Once you have logged in to the repository, you can push the image using the following command.

```
docker push <<image created above>>
```

You can validate this by going to `https://hub.docker.com` and checking the presence of the image (see Figure 7-4).

Figure 7-4. Docker repository with the Docker images of Rust and Golang web app

This completes the Docker side of the story. Now you need to deploy this Docker image onto a Kubernetes cluster.

Prerequisites

To deploy the Wasm modules created earlier, you need a Kubernetes cluster, such as Amazon Elastic Kubernetes Service (Amazon EKS) or Google Kubernetes Engine (GKE). You can also try this on a laptop using the minikube/Kubernetes offering.

As with Kubernetes, you create two resources: a pod and a service. You create two yaml files.

- For the pod

- For the Kubernetes service to expose the pod over a load balancer

The Pod Yaml File

Create a yaml file named rustexample.yaml, and copy the following content.

```
apiVersion: v1
kind: Pod
metadata:
  name: rust-example
  labels:
    role: rust-example
spec:
  containers:
    - name: web
      image: smjain/rustexample:latest
      ports:
        - name: web
          containerPort: 8080
          protocol: TCP
```

The image refers to the Docker image pushed to Docker Hub (smjain/rustexample).

The Rust web app is exposed as port 8080 on the host on which the Docker image runs.

The Service Yaml File

Create a yaml file named rustservice.yaml and copy the following content.

```
apiVersion: v1
kind: Service
metadata:
  name: rust-web-service
```

```
spec:
  type: LoadBalancer
  ports:
  - name: http
    port: 80
    targetPort: 8080
  selector:
    role: rust-example
```

The load balancer service type allows the web app to be consumed using the AWS load balancer in the example. If you intend to use minikube as the Kubernetes setup, go to https://kubernetes.io/docs/tutorials/hello-minikube/, or follow any other minikube tutorial.

Deploy the pod using the following command.

```
First create a namespace test
kubectl create namespace test
Create/Deploy the pod
kubectl apply -f rustexample.yaml --namespace test
Deploy the service using the below command
kubectl apply -f rustservice.yaml --namespace test

Pods can be checked by using the command
kubectl get pods --namespace test
```

```
root@INLN34327424A:/home/ubuntu# kubectl get pods --namespace test
NAME            READY    STATUS    RESTARTS    AGE
rust-example    1/1      Running   0           16m
```

Figure 7-5. *Pods in test namespace*

Service can be checked by using the following command.

```
kubectl get svc --namespace test
```

This creates a load balancer type of service which creates a network load balancer (in AWS), and the back end to the load balancer is the Rust-based app that you are running as a Docker container within a pod.

The HTTP request is proxied by the load balancer to the back end (Rust-based HTTP server in our case).

You can test the app by making a cURL request. The following HTTP URL is from the Kubernetes cluster I have created. You should replace it with your URL.

```
curl -d "name-foo" -X GET http://a14026b378049468c89f18868a933e44-
673171692.eu-central-1.elb.amazonaws.com
```

Here you provide key/value pair (name=foo), and since you can recall from our cuckoo Wasm module, foo is one of the entries present in the cuckoo filter, and therefore you get true as the answer.

When you try with a value like foo1, the service returns false as the answer.

The following is a scenario.

```
curl -d "name=foo" -X GET http://a14026b378049468c89f18868a933e44-
673171692.eu-central-1.elb.amazonaws.com
results in answer as true
```

This is another scenario.

```
curl -d "name=foo1" -X GET http://a14026b378049468c89f18868a933e44-
673171692.eu-central-1.elb.amazonaws.com
returns false as the answer
```

A Golang-based Web App Deployed on Kubernetes

The Golang-based web app uses the Wasmer engine for WebAssembly. This needs one additional change than the Rust-based web app, which is the libwasmer.so file. The specific version is made part of the GitHub project and can be taken from there.

More adventurous readers can install the Wasmer dependency on their machines and then extract the libwasmer.so file from there.

```
Install the wasmer dependency
go get github.com/wasmerio/wasmer-go/wasmer
```

You can find the libwasmer.so file at $GOPATH/pkg/mod/github.com/wasmerio/go-ext-wasm@v0.3.1/wasmer/.

```
$GOPATH/pkg/mod/github.com/wasmerio/go-ext-wasm@v0.3.1/wasmer/
```

To avoid version conflicts, it's advisable to take this library from GitHub for this book.

Create the Docker file as follows.

```
FROM golang:latest

RUN mkdir -p /app
WORKDIR /app
Add . /app
RUN go mod download
RUN go mod tidy
RUN go get github.com/wapc/wapc-go
RUN go get github.com/izinin/json2msgpack

RUN  LD_LIBRARY_PATH="/app/"
RUN go build -o main .

EXPOSE 8080
```

CMD

```
["./main","cuckoo_wapc.wasm","check_word_exists"]
```

In the Docker file, you should set the LD_LIBRARY_PATH to the libwasmer.so file to have the Wasmer dependency loaded by the executable you create.

Building the Docker file using the Docker build command shows the following output.

```
Step 3/12 : WORKDIR / app
---> Using cache
---> 81639c22f11f
Step 4/12 : Add . /app
---> 81f4479bbedc
Step 5/12 : RUN go mod download
---> Running in 0da 970b67fce
Removing intermediate container 0da 970b67fce
---> 7f1d28c92ec5
Step 6/12 : RUN go mod tidy
---> Running in a06abd4267a9
Removing intermediate container a06abd4267a9
---> 04a 906b 68 48a
Step 7/12 : RUN go get github.com/wapc/wapc-go
---> Running in 34 cea 66da01d
go: downloading github.com/wapc/wapc-go v0.3.0
go get: upgraded github.com/wapc/wapc-go v0.2.1 => v0.3.0
Removing intermediate container 34cea66da01d
---> b75d6701c544
Step 8/12 : RUN go get github.com/izinin/json2msgpack
---> Running in 9b2a05abed9f
Removing intermediate container 9b2a05abed9f
---> 663306c823b7
Step 9/12 : RUN LD_LIBRARY_PATH="/app/"
```

```
---> Running in f7d49afc76fa
Removing intermediate container f7d49afc76fa
---> 8a1491b3297a
Step 10/12 : RUN go build -o main.
---> Running in ac5504bef124
Removing intermediate container ac5504bef124
---> 3a8b2964544f
Step 11/12 : EXPOSE 8080
---> Running in fda06563256d
Removing intermediate container fda06563256d
---> 189433b6ca29
Step 12/12 : CMD ("./main","cuckoo_wapc.wasm", "check_word_exists"]
---> Running in 6e63d55f3986
Removing intermediate container 6e63d55f3986
---> 07edf39f79f7
Successfully built 07edf39f79f7
Successfully tagged smjain/goexample:latest
```

The Docker file passes two arguments.

- The Wasm file used for all the web apps

- The Wasm function name (check_word_exists)

You are tagging it as smjain/goexample. You can choose your own tag based on the Docker registry you use.

Once the build is done, you can check the container locally.

```
docker run -p 8080:8080  smjain/goexample
```

You can test this locally.

```
curl  -G -i "http://localhost:8080"--data-urlencode
'key={"name":"bar"}'
```

This should return true as the answer.

Kubernetes Deployment of the Golang Web App

Once you push the Docker image to Docker Hub, it's time to deploy it on Kubernetes.

Create two yaml files.

- For the pod

- For the Kubernetes service to expose the pod over a load balancer

The Pod Yaml File

Create a yaml file named goexample.yaml and copy the following content.

```
apiVersion: v1
kind: Pod
metadata:
  name: golang-example
  labels:
    role: golang-example
spec:
  containers:
    - name: web
      image: smjain/goexample:latest
      ports:
        - name: web
          containerPort: 8080
          protocol: TCP
```

The image refers to the Docker image you pushed to Docker Hub (smjain/rustexample).

The Rust web app is exposed as port 8080 on the host on which the Docker image runs.

The Service Yaml File

Create a yaml file named golangservice.yaml and copy the following content.

```
apiVersion: v1
kind: Service
metadata:
  name: go-web-service
spec:
  type: LoadBalancer
  ports:
  - name: http
    port: 80
    targetPort: 8080
  selector:
    role: golang-example
```

The load balancer service type allows the web app to be consumed using the AWS load balancer in the example.

Deploy the pod using the following command.

```
kubectl apply -f goexample.yaml --namespace test
Deploy the service using the below command
kubectl apply -f golangservice.yaml --namespace test
```

Pods can be checked by using the command.

```
kubectl get pods --namespace test
```

```
root@INLN34327424A:/home/ubuntu# kubectl get pods --namespace test
NAME              READY   STATUS    RESTARTS   AGE
golang-example    1/1     Running   0          56s
```

Figure 7-6. *Pods in namespace test*

You can check the services using the following command.

```
kubectl get svc –namespace test
```

On running cURL on the service URL(obtained from the above command)

```
curl -G -i "http://a8bd4a1ee42b0464db9643276640023a-1165927956.
eu-central-1.elb.amazonaws.com" --data-urlencode
'key={"name":"bar"}'
```

```
ubuntu@INLN34327424A:~$ curl -G -i "http://
a8bd4a1ee42b0464db9643276640023a-1165927956.eu-central-1.elb.
amazonaws.com" --data-urlencode 'key={"name":"bar"}'
HTTP/1.1 200 OK
Date: Tue, 03 Aug 2021 03:10:06 GMT
Content-Length: 5
Content-Type: text/plain; charset=utf-8
```

True

Try with an entry that doesn't exist.

```
ubuntu@INLN34327424A:~$ curl -G -i "http://
a8bd4a1ee42b0464db9643276640023a-1165927956.eu-central-1.elb.
amazonaws.com" --data-urlencode 'key={"name":"foo_x"}'
HTTP/1.1 200 OK
Date: Tue, 03 Aug 2021 03:12:26 GMT
Content-Length: 6
Content-Type: text/plain; charset=utf-8
```

False

149

The cuckoo filter Wasm module is now serving the HTTP request over the Kubernetes service.

Summary

In this chapter, you learned the basics of Docker and Kubernetes. You also learned how to make a web application, create a Docker file, and build a Docker image from it. In addition, you learned how to deploy this Docker file in Kubernetes and expose it over a load balancer. The service deployed on receipt of an HTTP request loads the Wasm module and invokes the function it exposes.

CHAPTER 8

Extending Istio with WebAssembly

This chapter looks at using WebAssembly in an Istio/Envoy API gateway scenario.

What Is Envoy?

First, let's talk about a few ways by which you can extend the functionality of Envoy. The Envoy proxy executes a variety of filters as part of an HTTP and TCP request process that provides features such as network routing, observability, and security.

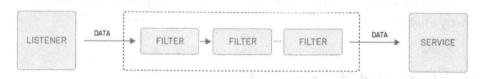

Figure 8-1. *Envoy filter chains for request processing*

Using these different filters, you can message individual TCP/HTTP requests. You can easily achieve things like updating headers, performing security checks like authentication, collecting stats, and so forth.

There are various prebuilt filters available, such as the envoy. filters.http.ratelimit filter that allows you to configure rate limiting for your services, the CSRF filter, the CORS filter, and more. You should always check the latest version to see what it supports before extending Envoy. However, you can also write your own filters and extend Envoy functionality.

Envoy also comes embedded with a V8 virtual machine (VM). V8 is a high-performance JavaScript and WebAssembly engine written in C++ and used in Chrome and Node.js (along with other applications and platforms). This engine allows you to deploy WebAssembly-based filters launched as part of the Envoy request processing pipeline.

Envoy operates using a multithreaded model. That means there's one main thread that is responsible for handling configuration updates and executing global tasks.

In addition to the main thread, there are also worker threads responsible for processing individual HTTP requests and TCP connections. The worker threads work on an event loop-based model and are independent of each other. The Envoy worker thread loads the Wasm module and executes it.

Envoy's more technical details are beyond the scope of this book.

Now, let's start creating a Rust-based Wasm filter that deploys on the Envoy engine.

Rust-based Wasm Filter

First, install Docker and Docker Compose on an Ubuntu machine. Then, create a Rust project named envoy_wasm using the following command.

```
cargo new envoy_wasm --lib
```

The following is the Cargo.toml file content.

```
[package]
name = "envoy_wasm"
version = "0.1.0"
edition = "2018"

# See more keys and their definitions at https://doc.rust-lang.
  org/cargo/reference/manifest.html

[dependencies]
log = "0.4.8"
proxy-wasm = "0.1.0" # The Rust SDK for proxy-wasm

[lib]
path = "src/lib.rs"
crate-type = ["cdylib"]
```

The src/lib.rs file has the following contents.

```
use log::info;
use proxy_wasm as wasm;

#[no_mangle]
pub fn _start() {
//    proxy_wasm::set_log_level(wasm::types::LogLevel::Trace);
    proxy_wasm::set_http_context(
        |context_id, _root_context_id| -> Box<dyn
        wasm::traits::HttpContext> {
            Box::new(HelloWorld { context_id })
        },
    )
}
```

```rust
struct HelloWorld {
    context_id: u32,
}

impl wasm::traits::Context for HelloWorld {}

impl wasm::traits::HttpContext for HelloWorld {
    fn on_http_request_headers(&mut self, num_headers: usize)
    -> wasm::types::Action {
        info!("Got {} HTTP headers in #{}.", num_headers,
        self.context_id);
        let headers = self.get_http_request_headers();
        let mut authority = "";

        for (name, value) in &headers {
            if name == ":authority" {
                authority = value;
            }
        }

        self.set_http_request_header("x-hello", Some(&format!
        ("Hello world from {}", authority)));

        wasm::types::Action::Continue
    }
}
```

This code prints the headers in the HTTP request.

```
Building the rust based wasm filter
cargo build --target wasm32-unknown-unknown --release
```

Once the Wasm file is built, it's time to deploy it to Envoy.

Deployment Steps

First, clone the Git repository at https://github.com/allthingssecurity/ rustenvoy in your directory by using the following command.

```
copy the envoy_wasm.wasm file to the rustenvoy/envoy directory
cp target/wasm32-unknown-unknown/release/envoy_wasm.wasm
rustenvoy/envoy
```

Envoy Setup

Let's use Istio Envoy v2 for loading and executing the Wasm module.

The following is the content of the Docker file in the envoy/Dockerfile. proxy directory.

```
FROM istio/proxyv2
#FROM yskopets/envoy-wasm:64d91b2
ENTRYPOINT /usr/local/bin/envoy -c /etc/envoy.yaml -l
debug --service-cluster proxy
```

The following is the Docker Compose file content.

```
version: '2'
services:

  proxy:
    build:
      context:  ./envoy
      dockerfile: Dockerfile.proxy
    volumes:
      - ./envoy/envoy.yaml:/etc/envoy.yaml
      - ./envoy/envoy_wasm.wasm:/etc/envoy_wasm.wasm
      # Uncomment this line if you want to use your own Envoy
        with WASM enabled.
```

```
#     - ./envoy/istio/envoy:/usr/local/bin/envoy
    networks:
      - envoymesh
    expose:
      - "80"
      - "8001"
    ports:
      - "18000:80"
      - "18001:8001"

  web_service:
    image: hashicorp/http-echo
    command:
      - '-text="You just ran wasm module within Istio/Envoy"'
    networks:
      envoymesh:
        aliases:
          - web_service
    expose:
      - "5678"
    ports:
      - "18080:5678"

networks:
  envoymesh: {}
```

This file starts two Docker containers: one for Envoy and one for an echo service proxied by Envoy. The echo service runs at port 5678, and Envoy listens at port 18000.

envoy.yaml located under the rustenvoy/envoy directory

```
static_resources:
  listeners:
  - name: main
```

```
address:
  socket_address:
    address: 0.0.0.0
    port_value: 80
filter_chains:
- filters:
  - name: envoy.http_connection_manager
    config:
      stat_prefix: ingress_http
      codec_type: auto
      route_config:
        name: local_route
        virtual_hosts:
        - name: local_service
          domains:
          - "*"
          routes:
          - match:
              prefix: "/"
            route:
              cluster: web_service
      http_filters:
      - name: envoy.filters.http.wasm
        config:
          config:
            name: "prime_auth"
            root_id: "prime_auth"
            vm_config:
              runtime: "envoy.wasm.runtime.v8"
              code:
                local:
```

```
                    filename: "/etc/envoy_wasm.wasm"
               allow_precompiled: true
        - name: envoy.router
          config: {}
- name: staticreply
  address:
    socket_address:
      address: 127.0.0.1
      port_value: 8099
  filter_chains:
  - filters:
    - name: envoy.http_connection_manager
      config:
        stat_prefix: ingress_http
        codec_type: auto
        route_config:
          name: local_route
          virtual_hosts:
          - name: local_service
            domains:
            - "*"
            routes:
            - match:
                prefix: "/"
              direct_response:
                status: 200
                body:
                  inline_string: "example body\n"
        http_filters:
        - name: envoy.router
          config: {}
```

```
clusters:
- name: web_service
  connect_timeout: 0.25s
  type: STRICT_DNS
  lb_policy: round_robin
  hosts:
  - socket_address:
      address: web_service
      port_value: 5678
admin:
  access_log_path: "/dev/null"
  address:
    socket_address:
      address: 0.0.0.0
      port_value: 8001
```

Launch Envoy

From the rustenvoy directory (where the Docker Compose file is located), run the following command.

```
docker-compose up --build
```

You should see Envoy and the echo service starting in their respective ports.

Once Envoy launches, create a cURL request to it using a separate console/shell.

```
curl  -H "name":"shashank" 0.0.0.0:18000
```

The preceding command injects an HTTP header with "name" as the name and "shashank" as the value.

On examining the console where Envoy is running, you see the following output and HTTP headers printed (shown in bold).

```
|  ':authority', '0.0.0.0:18000'
proxy_1        |  ':path', '/'
proxy_1        |  ':method', 'GET'
proxy_1        |  ':scheme', 'http'
proxy_1        |  'user-agent', 'curl/7.64.0'
proxy_1        |  'accept', '*/*'
proxy_1        |  'name', 'shashank'
proxy_1        |  'x-forwarded-proto', 'http'
proxy_1        |  'x-request-id', 'e971db8c-7b92-4734-a08f-
                   25e495d11e5b'
proxy_1        |  'x-envoy-expected-rq-timeout-ms', '15000'
```

Summary

In this chapter, you learned the basics of Envoy and how to install it on an Ubuntu machine using func e. You also learned how to use proxy-wasm to create Wasm-based filters for HTTP request processing in Envoy. Finally, you learned how to deploy the Wasm filters in Envoy.

This book began with an introduction to WebAssembly, discussing what it means for browsers and cloud-based applications. Later, it introduced wat (WebAssembly text format), allowing you to write WebAssembly modules in text format and translate it to a fully functional Wasm module. It also discussed tools like WaPC for handling complex types in Wasm modules.

You learned how to create a simple Wasm module based on the cuckoo filter and exposed it over an HTTP interface locally and remotely (by deploying it into the Kubernetes cluster). Finally, you learned how to use Wasm within Istio/Envoy by creating a simple HTTP filter Wasm module.

Overall, Wasm holds a lot of promise for the future of cloud and edge-based workloads.

Index

A

Address space randomized layout (ASRL), 23
Amazon Elastic Kubernetes Service (Amazon EKS), 140

B

Bloom filter, 72–76, 98

C

Cargo.toml file, 81, 93, 118
cgroups, 131
Cloud Native Computing Foundation, 3
Compute unit, 2
Container-based virtualization, 1
Cuckoo filters, 77, 84
cuckoo_http binary file, 127
cuckoo.wasm file, 82

D

Docker, 129, 130
Docker compose file, 136, 155
Docker images, 132, 139
Docker registry, 139, 146

E, F

Envoy, 151, 152, 154, 159
Envoy proxy, 151

G

Golang-based web app, 144, 145
golangservice.yaml, 148
Google Kubernetes Engine (GKE), 140
greetMe function, 61, 62, 66

H

Hash operations, 76
Homeostasis, 133
Hypervisor, 1

I, J

init() method, 99
Interoperable, 2, 4

K

Kubelet, 135
Kubernetes, 2, 73, 129, 132
Kubernetes cluster, 135, 140, 143, 160

Y, Z

Printed in the United States
by Baker & Taylor Publisher Services